NORTHEAST COMMUNITY COLLEGE LIBRARY

W9-BCW-177

WITHDRAWN

The Economics of Information

Library and Information Science Text Series

The School Library Media Center. 5th ed. By Emanuel T. Prostano and Joyce S. Prostano

Library and Information Center Management. 5th ed. By Robert D. Stueart and Barbara B. Moran

The Academic Library: Its Context, Its Purpose, and Its Operation. By John M. Budd

The Social Sciences: A Cross-Disciplinary Guide to Selected Sources. 2d ed. Nancy L. Herron, General Editor

Introduction to United States Government Information Sources. 6th ed. By Joseph Morehead

The Economics of Information: A Guide to Economic and Cost-Benefit Analysis for Information Professionals. 2d ed. By Bruce R. Kingma

Reference and Information Services: An Introduction. 3d ed. Richard E. Bopp and Linda C. Smith, General Editors

Developing Library and Information Center Collections. 4th ed. By G. Edward Evans with the assistance of Margaret R. Zarnosky

The Collection Program in Schools: Concepts, Practices, and Information Sources. 2d ed. By Phyllis J. Van Orden

Information Sources in Science and Technology. 3d ed. By C. D. Hurt

Introduction to Technical Services. 6th ed. By G. Edward Evans and Sandra M. Heft

The School Library Media Manager. 2d ed. By Blanche Woolls

The Humanities: A Selective Guide to Information Sources. 5th ed. By Ron Blazek and Elizabeth Aversa

Wynar's Introduction to Cataloging and Classification. 9th ed. By Arlene G. Taylor

Introduction to Library Public Services. 6th ed. By G. Edward Evans, Anthony J. Amodeo, and Thomas L. Carter

A Guide to the Library of Congress Classification. 5th ed. By Lois Mai Chan

The Organization of Information. By Arlene G. Taylor

Systems Analysis for Librarians and Information Professionals. 2d ed. By Larry N. Osborne and Margaret Nakamura

The Economics
of Information

**A Guide to Economic and Cost-Benefit
Analysis for Information Professionals**

Second Edition

Bruce R. Kingma

2001
Libraries Unlimited, Inc.
Englewood, Colorado

658.1554
K54e

Copyright © 2001 Bruce R. Kingma
All Rights Reserved
Printed in the United States of America

No part of this publication may be reproduced, stored in a re-
trieval system, or transmitted, in any form or by any means,
electronic, mechanical, photocopying, recording, or otherwise,
without the prior written permission of the publisher.

Libraries Unlimited, Inc.
P.O. Box 6633
Englewood, CO 80155-6633
1-800-237-6124
www.lu.com

Library of Congress Cataloging-in-Publication Data

Kingma, Bruce R.
    The economics of information : a guide to economic and cost-benefit analysis for
information professionals / Bruce R. Kingma.--2nd ed.
        p. cm. -- (Library and information science text series)
    Includes bibliographical references and index.
    ISBN 1-56308-816-9 (pbk.)
    1. Cost effectiveness. 2. Information science--Economic aspects. I. Title. II Series.

HD47.4 .K56 2001
658.15'54--dc21

00-050701

To Susan

Contents

Preface xi

Chapter 1: Introduction 1
Why Study Economics? 2
Economics 4
Information Economics 6
Summary 8
Notes 8

Chapter 2: Costs 9
Fixed and Variable Costs 10
Marginal, Average, and Total Costs 12
Opportunity Costs 18
Other Cost Definitions 20
Supply and Costs 21
Market Supply 24
Changes in Market Supply 25
Price Elasticity of Supply 25
Summary 27
Notes 28

Chapter 3: Benefits 29
Demand 30
Price 30
Changes in Demand 32
Price Elasticity of Demand 35
Consumer Surplus 40
Summary 43
Notes 43

Chapter 4: Markets 45
The Market Equilibrium 46
Changes in Demand and Supply 47
Economic Efficiency 51
Market Failure 53
Summary 55

Chapter 5: Information as a Public Good 57
Public Good Demand 58
Financing Public Goods 61
Information as a Public Good 63
Summary 64

Chapter 6: Externalities..65
    Negative Externalities 66
    Positive Externalities..68
    Balancing Positive and
        Negative Externalities 70
    Summary 72

Chapter 7: Monopolies..75
    Monopoly Demand..77
    Natural Monopolies..80
    Multi-Price Suppliers 85
    Summary 88

Chapter 8: Uncertainty and Risk..89
    Expectations and the
        Value of Information..90
    Asymmetrical Information
        and Markets 92
    Information Markets..95
        Insurance 96
        Education..97
        Other Information Markets..97
    Modeling Information Acquisition...98
    Summary 101
    Notes...101

Chapter 9: Commodity or Public Good 103
    Market for Books and Journals 104
    Information Markets..107
    Summary 110

Chapter 10: Pricing...113
    User Fees as Allocation Tools...114
    Marginal Cost of Pricing 117
    Financing Information Goods:
        Ramsey Prices 121
    Financing Information Goods:
        Value-Based Prices..123
    Summary 125
    Notes...125

Chapter 11: Time...127
    Measuring the Value of Time..128
        Measuring Opportunity Costs 129
        Value of Time Saved...130
        Consumer Surplus and Economic Cost......................................132

Congestion..133
Present Value..136
Summary 139
Notes..140

Chapter 12: Resource Sharing 141
Multiple Users of Information Resources 141
Opportunity Cost of Patron Time..147
Summary 149

Chapter 13: The Costs and Benefits of Digital Information 151
Cost of Access to Information..152
    Consumer Costs...152
    Producer and Intermediary Costs 154
Pricing of Digital Information..156
Summary 159

Chapter 14: Network Economics 161
Pricing of Electronic Journals 162
Role of Libraries in a
    Networked Environment 165
Summary 166

Bibliography...167
Index...175

Preface

Graduate students in Master of Business Administration, Public Administration, and Nonprofit Management programs are required to take a class in economics. However, only a handful of graduate students in Master of Library Science and Master of Information Science programs are exposed to economics. This is unfortunate because many individuals who become information managers, library directors, and information policymakers get their start with an M.L.S. or M.I.S. degree. This book is written to make up that deficiency by offering an introduction to economics resources for librarians and information professionals. In each chapter, basic economic concepts—demand, supply, benefits, costs—are presented, along with several examples to illustrate these concepts. Throughout this book, examples of information goods and services are used to explain the application of economics to information markets.

This book will be particularly valuable to individuals who are, or hope to be, managers of information services in academic, public, or special libraries and for those without a background in economics who plan to research the value and cost of information. The economic tools presented will help information professionals who are managers and policymakers to make better decisions. This book provides readers with an introduction to economics and cost-benefit analysis. After finishing this book, readers will have a better understanding of information markets, be able to understand economic research on information topics, and be able to complete basic cost-benefit analyses of information goods and services.

The first and second editions of this book evolved over the past 10 years from my lecture notes for "The Economics of Information Management" class in the M.L.S., M.I.S., and Ph.D. programs at the School of Information Science and Policy at the State University of New York at Albany. Although the economics of information continues to be one of the most controversial and popular topics for research in information science, this class is one of only a handful on this topic taught in information science programs. This book, written by an economist, provides an introduction to economics and cost-benefit analysis to those individuals who have not taken a class in the economics of information.

The focus of this book is on the economics of information goods and services, which are sufficiently different from other types of goods and services that a complete understanding of their differences is important to managers and policymakers. For example, information affects individuals other than those who directly consume and produce it. Print, digital, or broadcast information over radio or television can be shared by many individuals without decreasing its value or worth. Information goods and services frequently have high fixed costs of production and lower marginal costs of reproduction. Copyright and patent laws exist to protect the original owner of intellectual property while establishing the owner as the single supplier, or monopolist, of the information. Finally, those with information, such as mechanics or doctors, can exploit those without information by misrepresenting quality and costs, thereby creating the incentive for information markets about the quality of goods and services to be performed. Each of these characteristics of information is important in developing cost-benefit models of information goods and services.

The second edition of this book incorporates the many changes that have occurred in my course lectures over the past five years. These include a more detailed discussion of cost analysis in Chapter 2, uncertainty and risk in Chapter 8, pricing in Chapter 10, time in Chapter 11, and the addition of Chapters 13 and 14 on the costs and benefits of digital information and networks.

Chapters 1 through 4 provide an introduction to economics and cost-benefit analysis. Cost analysis is described in detail in Chapter 2, including the many definitions of costs. Chapter 2 shows how economic costs differ from accounting costs and introduces the important concept of opportunity costs. Chapter 3 describes benefit analysis and demand. Cost and benefit analyses in markets are combined in Chapter 4.

Chapters 5 through 8 describe the characteristics of information and how they may result in markets failing to produce outcomes that are in society's best interests. Information goods can be public goods or externalities, result in monopolies, and produce uncertainty and risk in markets. Each of these characteristics of information is described in these chapters.

Chapters 9 through 12 provide examples of economic modeling of information markets. Chapter 9 compares the commodity and public good models of information. Chapter 10 examines pricing of information goods and services. Included in Chapter 10 is an analysis of pricing of information goods based on the value consumers receive from these goods rather than the cost of producing them. Chapter 11 introduces the opportunity cost of time in consuming information goods and the present value of future expenditures in cost-benefit analysis of information services. Chapter 12 examines resource sharing, an important topic in the current climate of library consortiums and collaborations.

Chapter 13 examines the costs and benefits of digital information. In this chapter the costs of digitization, print, and microfiche are compared to determine which is most cost effective. Chapter 14 examines the economics of networked digital information and provides a provocative analysis of scholarly journal pricing in the networked digital environment.

I would like to thank my students for helping me with this book and fine-tuning my lectures on this topic. I also would like to thank my wife, Susan, and my children, Patrick, Sabra, and George, for being patient with me during the completion of this book.

Chapter 1

Introduction

Information managers make economic decisions every day. Each decision is a choice among competing alternatives. For example, a manager must choose how to allocate a fixed budget among staff, supplies, computers, rent, and other possible expenditures. Spending more money in one expense category results in less to spend in another. For example, a manager must choose whether to purchase a new computer or a new photocopier. The local public library director may decide to open the library on Sundays. The extra money spent on staff and utilities to keep the library open could have been spent purchasing more books.

Economics examines how these decisions are made and which alternatives provide the greatest benefit to the various stakeholders, people or groups with an interest in the decision. Each decision has costs and benefits associated with it. Economics provides a set of tools to measure these costs and benefits, thereby enabling managers to make better decisions. These tools are demand, supply, costs, and benefits. This book examines how to measure these.

Economics is defined as the study of the allocation of scarce resources. Economists assume that resources are limited and must be allocated to satisfy insatiable wants. Scarce resources include a library budget, personal income, or the federal budget. Scarce resources can also be office space, employees, time, books, computers, digital storage space, bandwidth, or shelf space. In each example there is a fixed amount of the resource that must be used by stakeholders. Allocating these resources means determining how to use, spend, or divide them, in other words, how to spend the library budget or your personal budget, allocate the office space, schedule employees' time, loan books, give the computers to employees, divide the digital storage space among various digital records, divide shelf space among collections of books, or allocate bandwidth to digital requests for files. In each case choices must be made about the best use of limited resources.

Each alternative use of resources provides different benefits to various stakeholders. Economists quantify these benefits to determine the best allocation of the resources or goods. Purchasing a photocopier means forgoing the purchase of a new computer. The benefits of the photocopier must be compared to the forgone benefits of the computer. Likewise, each allocation in a budget produces benefits of purchases at the cost of forgone benefits from alternative purchases. The benefits and costs from a set of purchases must be compared to the benefits and costs of alternative purchase decisions.

For information professionals, these decisions can be difficult. Information goods and services have different economic properties than do typical goods and services. The economics of books in a library, journal publishing, computer networks, and digital libraries are different from the economics of classic consumer goods such as butter and guns. Information goods and services are sometimes shared with other consumers, can be consumed with or without purchase, cannot be easily returned, require laws that protect monopoly rights, and lock in consumers to suppliers. These properties make information economics different from other forms of economics.

Why Study Economics?

Economics provides tools to analyze management and policy decisions. These tools help in making efficient decisions about the allocation of resources. For example, suppose a library director receives an increase of $100,000 to her budget for this and all future years. Should she use the new resources to hire additional librarians, hire additional clerical staff, purchase books, purchase computers, or choose some combination of these four alternatives? What guidelines should she use to make these decisions?

Suppose the corporate information manager must allocate five new computers among 10 employees. Who should get a new computer? Should he give the new computers to the employees with the oldest computers or to the employees with the most seniority, or use some other rule to allocate the computers?

Finally, suppose a foundation grants officer is responsible for distributing $10 million in grants to libraries that have submitted proposals outlining how they would use the money to provide Internet access for patrons. Should the grants officer give the money to the organizations serving the neediest populations, those with the greatest likelihood of success with providing access, those with the greatest potential for long-run financial stability, or those with the least financial stability?

Economics—or more specifically, cost-benefit analysis—provides a set of theoretical and empirical tools for making the best choices in each of these circumstances. The director, manager, or grants officer must weigh the costs and benefits of each alternative. If the benefits of an alternative exceed the costs, it is *economically efficient.* Options that provide the greatest net benefit are the most economically efficient. If the costs exceed the benefits, the alternative is *economically inefficient.*

Although it is not the only way to evaluate management and policy decisions, economics provides an unbiased, objective method of analysis. Economists avoid such value statements as "there should be free public library service for all," "there should be open access to government information," or "there should be universal access to telecommunications." Instead, economists use a ledger of costs and benefits for each possible decision.

For example, we know that public libraries provide significant benefits to the communities they serve. However, these benefits come at a cost. Taxpayer dollars must be used to support the building, staffing, and materials needed for the public library. If the benefits to the community are greater than the costs, it is economically efficient to provide financial support to the public library. Economics can also help determine the level of efficient financial support by measuring the increased benefit from increased library service and comparing it to the increased cost. Open access to government information provides the benefit of an informed electorate and makes it easier for individuals and businesses to get needed information from the government. The benefit of an informed electorate may prevent poor policy making by elected officials or enable the voters to more easily identify incompetent politicians. The costs of open access to government include the financial costs of storing, organizing, reproducing, and distributing government documents. Open access to government documents might also reveal state secrets, jeopardizing national security, or might reveal personal secrets, harming or embarrassing individuals and violating their rights to privacy. Therefore, access to government information may need to be restricted. Universal access to telecommunications has the benefit of providing individuals, businesses, and governments with a network that provides a connection to everyone. Likewise, there are benefits to individuals of having telephone access to friends, family, stores, and government offices. The cost of providing universal service is the added cost of wire and labor needed to connect each household to the network.

Economics is more than accounting. Accounting provides the numbers necessary for cost-benefit analysis but does not provide the tools of analysis. Managerial accounting—which includes break-even analysis, cost analysis, and performance analysis—provides some of the tools to analyze costs. However, economics provides additional tools such as the concepts of demand, marginal benefit, and consumer surplus, and the cost analysis tools of supply, marginal cost, and producer surplus, enabling managers and policymakers to decide how to spend a budget efficiently or implement policy. Economists also use these tools to forecast the effects of policy or the efficiency of management decisions.

Economics identifies the benefits and costs of decisions and weighs these against the benefits and costs of alternative decisions. Consumers enjoy identifiable benefits from the use of goods and services, while producers spend identifiable costs on the production of a good or provision of a service. When a library director considers keeping the library open an extra hour, he weighs the costs of staff and utilities against the benefits patrons might receive. The library director must also consider the potential benefit of using these resources on other services such as more books, computers, or more staff. When a publisher considers launching another journal title, she weighs the costs of editing, typesetting, printing, and distributing against the revenues received from sales. When policymakers consider imposing taxes on Internet commerce, they weigh the costs of decreased sales and a decline in economic activity against the added government revenue from the tax and the potential services that this revenue might finance. In each example, economics gives us the tools to analyze these alternatives, quantify the benefits and costs, and determine the most economically efficient choice.

Examples throughout this book demonstrate the usefulness of economic analysis in management and policy decisions. In most of these examples, the economic models are explained using fictitious numbers to give the reader the calculations behind the cost-benefit analyses. Cost-benefit analyses of information markets presented here include, among others, telephone service, academic library journal subscription policies, junk mail legislation, journal pricing, and digital information markets.

Economics

Economics is a social science. It examines how individuals and groups behave and interact in markets. Economists use mathematical models to quantify the benefits and costs of individual and group decisions and make unbiased, scientific assessments of value. These models help forecast markets and enable managers and policymakers to make economically efficient decisions.

Sometimes a manager's perception of the benefits and costs is enough to make the right decision even though these benefits and costs have not been explicitly measured. For example, if the library budget for collection development increases, it may be enough for the acquisitions librarian to subscribe to the additional journals she feels will best serve the library. This may be based on the opinions of a few patrons who have requested those journal titles. In this case, it may be relatively simple to determine which journals to purchase. The librarian simply assumes that the value to the patrons of requested journals exceeds the value of other journals for which no requests have been made.

At other times, it is important to explicitly calculate the benefits and costs of a policy or management decision. Several journal titles may have been requested and, with limited resources, the librarian must determine which titles will provide the most benefit for their costs. There may be more than one type of photocopier, computer, shelving, or online service provider. In each case, management decisions will be based on which photocopier, computer, shelving, or online service provides the most benefit for its cost.

Quantifying costs and benefits can be difficult. The cost of developing a new web site, the programming cost for a new computer software program, the cost of a universal telephone service, and the cost of staff development and training on a new computer system can be difficult to quantify. Benefits are even more difficult to measure than costs. It would be difficult to measure the benefits of a new company web site, the potential revenue from a new software program, the benefits of staff training on a new computer system, or the benefits of universal telephone service. The new company web site may increase sales or the value of company stock. A new software program may have the potential for new sales. The new computer system may make staff faster and more productive. However, until the system is installed and staff trained, it is difficult to measure the benefit from it. Even after the system is installed there may be benefits from additional training or system upgrades. In each example the economist must guess at the potential for new revenues or benefits.

The benefit from universal telephone service is also difficult to calculate. Individuals who cannot afford a telephone would benefit from communications access previously unavailable to them. Those who can afford a telephone would also benefit by having telephone access to more individuals than before. Schools would gain access to the parents of all pupils, government agencies would gain access to more clients, businesses would acquire access to more potential consumers, and all households would have immediate access to emergency services. However, it is difficult to quantify or measure these benefits. Yet to assume that universal telephone service is a worthwhile objective is to assume that these benefits are greater than the costs.

As a science, economics attempts to quantify the benefits and costs of universal telephone service without prejudging whether such an objective is "good" or "bad." Rather than taking sides in the debate of whether telephone or other information services are a fundamental right or whether those services should only go to those who pay for them, the science of economics simply determines if there is a net benefit from a policy. Of course, the measurement of benefits and costs may be debatable depending on the individual economist's view of what items belong on which side of the ledger, the relative value placed on each benefit, and the underlying assumptions of the economic model. However, all economists use the same set of economic tools—demand, supply, marginal cost, and marginal benefit—to make their calculations.

Economics is also the study of human behavior. The cornerstone of economic models of human behavior is the assumption that individuals behave rationally in ways they believe give them the most net benefit. Everyone goes through life facing choices—Should I become a lawyer or a librarian? Should I purchase a new car or fix the old one? Should I read a novel or watch television?—and individuals make their choices based on what they believe will provide them with the most benefit. Susan may decide to have her car fixed rather than purchase a new car because she expects that the repairs will cost less and last a sufficient period of time to get the maximum net benefit from the old car. Additionally, Susan may not have the savings to or be able to get a loan from the bank to purchase a new car, or may simply have a nostalgic attachment to the old car. Economics is used to explain human behavior based on the rational choices of individuals acting in their own self-interest.

Given the assumption of rational behavior, economic tools have proven remarkably useful and reliable in studying not only traditional markets but also such diverse information markets as drugs, crime, marriage, fertility, charity, and religion. For example, teenage pregnancy is related to teenage perceptions of the chance of pregnancy, standard of living, education, job opportunities, and information about preventing pregnancy. A teenager considering having sexual relations is making a fundamentally economic choice, comparing the benefits of his or her action with the potential costs of pregnancy, disease, and reputation. Accurate information provided at home or at school may influence a teenager's perception of the risks or costs associated with sexual relations and therefore may decrease the number of unwanted pregnancies.[1]

Another arena in which people make economic choices is the marriage market. Courtship is the process of collecting information on the likelihood of a beneficial match between oneself and another. Marriage is a legal agreement in which both parties agree to stop collecting information on other potential mates. Divorce is the acknowledgment by one or both parties that incomplete information was collected during courtship.[2] Similarly, the market for religion is a market for information. Religious leaders must convince their congregations that they have a set of religious beliefs that will lead to salvation. Each religious leader "sells" to the congregation information about salvation.[3]

Information markets are possible because individuals want to acquire information to help them make decisions under uncertain conditions. Acquiring information on the weather, consumer products, movie reviews, and company performance helps individuals make better choices about whether to carry an umbrella, purchase a new car, rent a video, or invest in a stock.

The science of economics uses theories and models of costs and benefits to explain and examine human behavior. Any action by a manager, policymaker, patron, or client will result in costs and benefits to a set of stakeholders. Consumers purchase goods because they believe the benefits from those purchases will outweigh the costs, and suppliers believe the revenue they receive will outweigh the costs of production. Economics, as a science, uses the theories of consumer behavior (demand) and producer behavior (supply) to explain market transactions.

Information Economics

The economics of information is different in several ways from the economics of classic goods and services. Classic goods and services include cars, restaurant meals, or pencils. The classic example of a pencil includes the trade for the basic inputs of a pencil—eraser, wood, graphite, tin—to a single producer that manufactures and sells pencils. The price of a pencil is based on the cost of combining these goods into a single good and selling it at the cost of inputs, including the labor needed to manufacture it and the return on the entrepreneur's investment in the pencil factory. With each 20-cent pencil the consumer is paying for the costs of making it plus a small profit to the supplier. Likewise, the price of the restaurant meal or the car is similarly related to the costs of producing another restaurant meal or car.

Information has several properties that make information goods and services different from other goods and services. Information has large fixed costs of producing the first unit and relatively lower marginal costs for producing additional units. The value of information depends on when it is sold. Information when sold is still retained by the seller; information when purchased cannot be easily returned. And information can be enjoyed by more than one consumer without a decrease in the amount produced. In fact, in networked information markets the more consumers engaged in the market, the more benefit each consumer receives from it.

Producing books, music, movies, computer software, and other information goods involves large fixed costs for the first unit relative to additional units. The author must write the book and the publisher must have it edited and marketed before the first copy is sold. The artist must record the music, the movie must be filmed, and the software program must be written. In each case, there are large fixed costs of authors, artists, and programmers that must be paid for. Each unit of information sold comes at a relatively lower cost of production. An additional copy of a book, video, or CD has a cost of only a few dollars.

The value of information depends on its age and the time it is sold. Newer information tends to have more value. Instant information on the value of stocks has more benefit to a stockbroker than two-day-old information. Expedient delivery of information on someone's medical condition, research reports, the weather conditions, the news, or legal information is more valuable. Older information has less value. Information has more value when sold at the time it is produced.

Once sold, the information is still retained by the seller. When a researcher produces information for her employer she retains the knowledge of the research. If she were to leave the firm she works for she cannot leave research results but retains all the knowledge she gained during her employment. Similarly, information once purchased cannot be easily returned. If you buy a ticket to a movie, the viewing of it cannot be returned. Asking for your money back because you disliked the movie can be difficult. You cannot return the information.

The same information can be enjoyed by more than one consumer simultaneously. More than one person can enjoy a movie in a theater at the same time. More than one person can read the same book, view the same television program, use the same web site, and listen to the same music at the same time. This property of information makes it a public or shared good.

When individuals consume information on a telephone network or the Internet, the same information can be enjoyed by more than one consumer simultaneously. In addition, the use of the network increases the benefit from the information to all consumers. The greater the number of networked individuals, the more benefit from the network. The more individuals you can connect to a telephone network, the more benefit the network has for you. The more web sites you can visit on the Internet, the more benefit the network provides to you.

The properties of information result in markets different from classic economic markets. The classic models of demand and supply have to be modified for information goods and services. Information markets have properties of public goods, externalities, and monopolies that result in the need for government intervention, at times, to improve market performance and increase economic efficiency.

Summary

Economics provides a useful set of tools to examine information markets. These tools include costs, benefits, demand, and supply. Economics is useful to management and policymakers because it provides an unbiased way of examining decisions. Economists define the stakeholders of a decision and measure the costs and benefits of the alternatives on the stakeholders. If the benefits are greater than the costs, an alternative is efficient.

Information goods and services have characteristics that make these goods and services different from classic economic goods. These characteristics are examined throughout this book. The differences in information goods and services result in information markets having different characteristics from other markets. Information goods are likely to be public or shared goods, have externalities, or result in monopolies where one firm dominates the market. In addition, network effects increase the value of information goods and services.

These characteristics of information markets may result in the need for government financing or intervention. Governments may provide financing for information goods and services such as public libraries, medical research, education, or funding for the Internet infrastructure. Governments may regulate information markets such as telecommunications, television, software encryption, or computer operating systems. In each case, the need for government intervention must be carefully weighed against the potential of the market to self-correct any inefficiencies.

Notes

1. See Gary S. Becker, *A Treatise on the Family* (Cambridge, MA: Harvard University Press, 1991).

2. See Elizabeth Peters, "Marriage and Divorce: Informational Constraints and Private Contracting," *American Economic Review* (1986): 237-54.

3. See Laurence R. Iannaccone, "Sacrifice and Stigma: Reducing Free-Riding in Cults, Communes, and Other Collectives," *Journal of Political Economy* 100, no. 2 (1992): 271-91; and Laurence R. Iannaccone, "The Consequences of Religious Market Structure: Adam Smith and the Economics of Religion," paper in *Political Economy Report,* University of Western Ontario, 1991.

Chapter 2

Costs

To produce output an organization must purchase and combine inputs. The cost of producing a unit of output is the combined costs of the inputs necessary to make it. Nonprofit, for-profit, and government organizations must pay for labor, land, rent, construction, computers, supplies, telecommunications, legal services, administration, and other inputs to produce goods and services. The total costs of goods and services are the sum of the costs of the inputs used in production. The cost per unit is the simple division of this total cost by the number of units. These are basic, straightforward definitions of an organization's cost structure.

Information on an organization's costs includes more than total and average cost calculations. Several definitions of costs are helpful in understanding an organization, how costs might change if output changes, and the market supply of a good or service and how this supply is related to costs.

The behavior of an organization and its cost structure are determined by organizational goals. The goals of a firm determine how managers in that organization decide on the level of output, given the costs and productivity of inputs and the profitability, social value, or other perceived benefits of outputs. A for-profit firm produces output to make a profit; its goal is to maximize profit. Nonprofit firms and government organizations typically produce a good or service, maximizing the social value of that output. Nonprofit firms and government organizations do not produce to make a profit. Either type of organization may produce to maximize societal value, government employment, the best interests of a stakeholder, or the budget of an agency. In each case, it is important to quantify the costs, the amount and types of outputs, and the amount and types of inputs.

Fixed and Variable Costs

The cost of an output can be divided into two types: fixed costs and variable costs. Fixed costs do not change as the level of output changes. Regardless of the level of production, within a specified time period, fixed costs cannot be changed. In publishing, fixed costs are sometimes referred to as set-up costs, overhead, or first-copy costs. The cost of a factory or a library building is a fixed cost. Regardless of the amount of output or number of patrons served, the cost of a factory or library building is unchanged within the year. In publishing, the cost of the author's or editor's time is fixed within a month. Fixed costs for universities include the cost of the university network, buildings, and administration.

Variable costs increase as the level of output increases within a given period of time. The costs of employees and many types of supplies are typically variable costs. For a publisher, variable costs include the cost of paper, printing, and shipping. As more books are produced, more of these supplies must be purchased. Hourly wages paid to employees are variable costs. In a library, to increase library services, computer user room hours, or telephone help services, employee hours must increase. To increase the number of copies made on a photocopy machine, the amount of paper and toner purchased must be increased.

Fixed and variable costs are defined by the output and the period of time chosen. If the goal is to increase production over the next month, variable costs are those that can realistically be changed within that time period. Over a longer period of time, more costs are variable. Skilled labor is frequently a fixed cost in a month, but given a longer period of time it can become a variable cost. It may take several months to hire and train information specialists in a corporate information department or library to the level at which they can be considered fully productive. In a month, salaries of corporate information employees may be a fixed cost in the production of services. However, given a year, more staff can be hired and trained; therefore, their salaries are variable costs given the longer time period.

For any particular good or service, there is usually a "common sense" division of fixed and variable costs and period of time for production. Inputs fixed for one good are more naturally defined as variable for another. For example, the author's time and first-copy costs in publishing a book are fixed costs, which must be incurred regardless of the number of copies that will be printed and sold. The printing of individual copies of the book is a variable cost. To print more copies, more paper, ink, and labor must be used. This provides a logical split of fixed and variable costs for production of a book title over a one- to three-month period.

However, over a longer time period the author's time and set-up costs can become variable costs. Over a year, a publisher can hire other authors to write additional book titles and incur additional set-up costs for each new title. Over a year, publishers make decisions about not only how many copies of individual titles to produce but also how many titles. Authors, editors, and set-up costs that were fixed over a period of a few months become variable over a year. However, it would still be difficult for a publisher to construct and occupy a building in a year, so the building may still reasonably be classified as a fixed cost. If the time period were increased to five years, then all costs would likely be variable.

Table 2.1 provides several examples of fixed and variable costs for information goods and services. In each case, fixed inputs and variable inputs must be combined to produce units of output. Although fixed inputs must be employed to start production, variable inputs must be purchased to increase the production of the output within the time period. For longer time periods, more costs become variable.

Table 2.1
Fixed and Variable Costs of Production

Goods and Services	Time Period	Fixed Inputs	Variable Inputs
Copies of a novel	One month	Editing, author's time, office space	Ink, toner, labor, shipping
Book publishing	One year	Office space	Printing, distributing, authors' time, set-up costs
College courses	One week	Space, faculty, equipment	Students' time, papers
College courses	One semester	Space, equipment, tenured faculty	Untenured or adjunct faculty, students' time, papers
Computer software	One month	Space, programmer's time	Copies of program, compact disks, packaging
Library books	One semester	Space, library administration, librarians	Books, circulation staff, unskilled labor
Telephone service	One day	Telephone, telecommunications network	Operator assistance, electricity
Television program	One hour	Studio space, cameras, labor, television	Electricity

Goods and Services	Time Period	Fixed Inputs	Variable Inputs
Television programs	One year	Studio space	Cameras, labor, television, electricity
Digital images	One day	Space, server, labor, scanner, Web development, computers, network	Patrons' time spent viewing the documents
Digital library	One year	Space	Server, labor, scanner, Web development, computers, network, patrons' time
Commercial web site	One month	Space, server, Web design, products, administration	Some parts of the Web design, some products, distribution costs

Marginal, Average, and Total Costs

Variable costs are costs that can be changed. The marginal cost is the cost that results from increasing output by one unit. Marginal costs are the costs of variable inputs that must be employed to increase output. For example, the marginal cost of an additional copy of a computer program, to the producer of the program, is about $1.00 or the cost of pressing one more CD. The marginal cost of an additional hour of reference services at the library is the hourly wage of a reference librarian. The marginal cost of a copy of a book, to the publisher, is the cost of paper and ink used in printing one more copy.

Marginal costs, like variable costs, are determined by the period of time used. If a publisher is considering marginal costs of publishing additional books in a year, more costs are not fixed and can be changed. The marginal cost of books over a year includes the costs of hiring additional authors and editors. The marginal cost of digital images over a year includes the cost of scanning and publishing these images on a web page.

The average cost of a unit of output is the total cost divided by the number of units. The average cost is the cost per unit of output. Average total costs include fixed costs such as administration, overhead, and building costs that are not typically included in variable or marginal costs.

Table 2.2 illustrates the total, average, and marginal costs of a five-day computer class at Computer Horizons, a fictitious computer training school. The costs shown are incurred by Computer Horizons. The example illustrated in Table 2.2 assumes that each student needs $80 in software and supplies for the class. There is no assumption that Computer Horizons or the student is paying the $80, only that software and supplies must be purchased for each student. Other costs include the instructor's weekly salary of $1,000 and the costs of the equipment and space in the classroom of $500 per week. The class size may be limited by the space, the number of workstations in the room, or the company's restrictions. Table 2.2 assumes that there is a limit of 12 students per class. Computer Horizons is committed to offering one section of this class and therefore has fixed costs of $1,500. If 13 students want to take this class, a second section must be opened.

Table 2.2
Computer Horizons' Cost Schedule

Students (Output)	Fixed Cost	Variable Cost	Total Cost	Average Cost	Marginal Cost
0	$1,500	0	$1,500		
1	$1,500	$80	$1,580	$1,580	$80
2	$1,500	$160	$1,660	$830	$80
3	$1,500	$240	$1,740	$580	$80
4	$1,500	$320	$1,820	$455	$80
5	$1,500	$400	$1,900	$380	$80
6	$1,500	$480	$1,980	$330	$80
7	$1,500	$560	$2,060	$294	$80
8	$1,500	$640	$2,140	$268	$80
9	$1,500	$720	$2,220	$247	$80
10	$1,500	$800	$2,300	$230	$80
11	$1,500	$880	$2,380	$216	$80
12	$1,500	$960	$2,460	$205	$80
13	$1,500	$2,540	$4,040	$311	$1,580
14	$1,500	$2,620	$4,120	$294	$80

Computer Horizons has a marginal cost of $80 per student for each of the first 12 students. If 13 students want to take this class, and Computer Horizons is willing to open a second section, then the marginal cost for the thirteenth student is $1,580. This amount is the $80 for the software and supplies for this student plus the additional cost of an instructor and equipment for a second section. Once Computer Horizons agrees to offer a second section, then the marginal or additional costs of a fourteenth student are only the $80 in software and supplies needed for that student.

Figure 2.1 shows the average and marginal costs for the Computer Horizons class. As the number of students increases, the average cost per student decreases, until the thirteenth student. The marginal cost remains constant at $80, until the thirteenth student.

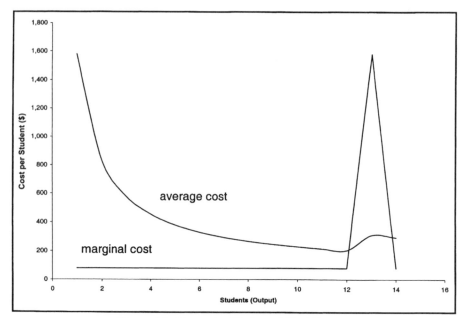

Figure 2.1. Computer Horizons' Cost Curves.

Average and marginal costs are important concepts in economics. These two types of costs are useful in determining how much is spent on each unit of output or customer served and, therefore, how much revenue must be made on each unit of output or customer to cover costs. For example, assume that Computer Horizons decides to charge $300 for each student to take this computer class. (This class fee includes the $80 cost of software and supplies.) The potential revenue and profit for Computer Horizons depends on the number of students who take this class. Table 2.3 shows the total revenue and profit as well as the average, marginal, and total costs from Table 2.2.

Table 2.3 Computer Horizons' Profit Schedule					
Students (Output)	Average Cost	Marginal Cost	Total Cost	Total Revenue	Profit (Loss)
0			$1,500		($1,500)
1	$1,580	$80	$1,580	$300	($1,280)
2	$830	$80	$1,660	$600	($1,060)
3	$580	$80	$1,740	$900	($840)
4	$455	$80	$1,820	$1,200	($620)
5	$380	$80	$1,900	$1,500	($400)
6	$330	$80	$1,980	$1,800	($180)
7	$294	$80	$2,060	$2,100	$40
8	$268	$80	$2,140	$2,400	$260
9	$247	$80	$2,220	$2,700	$480
10	$230	$80	$2,300	$3,000	$700
11	$216	$80	$2,380	$3,300	$920
12	$205	$80	$2,460	$3,600	$1,140
13	$311	$1,580	$4,040	$3,900	($140)
14	$294	$80	$4,120	$4,200	$80

Note: Numbers are rounded to the nearest dollar.

As long as the price or revenue per student of $300 exceeds the average cost per student there will be a positive profit. Profit equals the price minus the average cost per student multiplied by the number of students. At this price, if Computer Horizons expects 14 students or fewer to take this class, the company will achieve maximum revenue at 12 students.

As long as the price or revenue per student of $300 exceeds the marginal cost per student, Computer Horizons will make a profit on letting an additional student into the class. For each of the first 12 students the price of $300 and the cost of $80 meant that the company made $240 profit on that student. However, the thirteenth student requires opening an additional section of the class at a marginal cost of $1,580. At a price of $300 and a cost of $1,580, the company will loose $1,280 if it opens a second section of this class for only one student.

Most companies have more complex cost structures than this example. Typically, an organization has several categories of fixed and variable costs. Increasing output involves increasing overtime, hiring more employees, consuming more supplies and raw materials, and changing other costs. As more employees are hired or are asked to work overtime in the short run, the building space, administration, and other fixed factors must be used to serve more of the variable inputs. As more variable inputs are employed, the result is a congestion of the fixed factors of production. The result is what economists call the diminishing marginal productivity of the variable factors of production.

Diminishing marginal productivity can be illustrated with a simple example. Consider Software Games, Inc., a fictitious company that produces inexpensive computer games on compact disks. Software Games, Inc., employs a manager and programmers to produce a software game. Software Games, Inc., also has one CD press that can make 1,000 disks in a week if used 40 hours. The manager, programmers, and CD press are fixed factors of production. Assume that the total fixed costs of production are $10,000 per week. Software Games, Inc., also purchases supplies including compact disks and employs staff to press the computer game on CDs and distribute the copies. The supplies, compact disks, and staff for production and distribution are variable factors of production. Software Games, Inc., weekly production costs are illustrated in Table 2.4.

Table 2.4
Software Games, Inc., Weekly Cost Schedule

CDs Produced	Fixed Costs	Variable Costs	Total Cost	Average Cost per CD	Marginal Cost per CD
0	$5,000	0	$5,000		
500	$5,000	$1,500	$6,500	$13.00	$3.00
1,000	$5,000	$2,900	$7,900	$7.90	$2.80
1,500	$5,000	$4,600	$9,600	$6.40	$3.40
2,000	$5,000	$6,700	$11,700	$5.85	$4.20
2,500	$5,000	$9,300	$14,300	$5.72	$5.20
3,000	$5,000	$12,500	$17,500	$5.83	$6.40
3,500	$5,000	$16,400	$21,400	$6.11	$7.80
4,000	$5,000	$21,100	$26,100	$6.53	$9.40

As more disks are pressed, more staff must be employed, and existing staff must work overtime to increase output. A single CD press cannot make more than 1,000 disks in a 40-hour week. Late shifts must be added to use the press more hours per day. But as the press is used more, it is more susceptible to breaking down. The time the press cannot be used during repairs results in paid staff working but not producing more disks. As a result of adding more variable inputs of production to the fixed inputs, the increase in production from additional staff is lower than before. This declining marginal productivity of the variable factors implies that the marginal cost and, eventually, the average cost per unit of output increases. Within one week, Software Games, Inc., is not able to purchase an additional press to relieve the congestion of staff using the single press. The Software Games, Inc., cost schedule in this situation is shown in Figure 2.2.

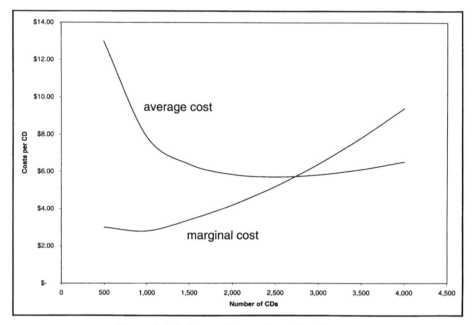

Figure 2.2. Software Games, Inc., Cost Curves.

Figure 2.2 illustrates classic economic cost curves for most goods and services. Frequently, production of goods and services depends on variable factors using fixed factors that can become congested if production is increased. This results in a declining marginal productivity and increasing marginal cost as output is increased.

Many information goods and services have a different cost structure from that of classic economic goods. Information goods have high fixed costs and relatively low marginal costs. Fixed costs include software development, authors' and editors' salaries, set-up or first copy costs, web page design and development, computer and communications network infrastructure, and research and development. Once these large expenses are incurred, there is a relatively lower marginal cost of reproducing the information. The costs of printing a book or newspaper, pressing a CD or floppy disk, accessing a web page, or using a company's intranet are trivial relative to the fixed costs of these goods and services.

Using the previous example, assume that Software Games' costs are considered over a one-month period instead of a one-week period. This may be sufficient time for this company to hire additional staff, purchase additional CD presses, or outsource the pressing of disks to another company. Assume that variable costs are a flat $1,500 per 500 disks or a marginal cost of $3.00 per disk. According to the example, Software Games, Inc., has fixed costs of $5,000 per week or $20,000 per month. The cost curves for Software Games, Inc., in this example are shown in Figure 2.3.

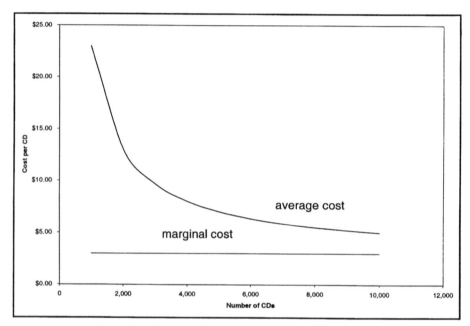

Figure 2.3. Software Games, Inc., Monthly Cost Curves.

In this example, Software Games' monthly cost curves show a continuously declining average cost and a constant marginal cost. As output increases, the portion of fixed costs that each unit of output shares declines while the marginal cost remains small and constant.

Digital information products delivered over a network are an extreme example of a declining average cost and low marginal cost. The marginal cost of downloading a copy of a software program is zero. The only cost is the time and effort the patron or customer must spend to download and learn how to use the software program.

Opportunity Costs

One of the most important tools that economic models offer to managers and policymakers is the notion of the opportunity cost of a good or service. *Opportunity cost* is the highest value of alternative opportunities forgone by consuming a good or service. Opportunity costs differ from financial or monetary costs because they include not only the money spent purchasing a good but also the value of time spent and opportunities lost when a good or service is consumed. For example, the opportunity cost of going to see a movie is the price of the movie ticket plus the value of the time spent watching the movie. The opportunity cost of reading a book is the price of the book plus the value of the time spent reading it. Even if the good does not have a monetary cost, it may still have an opportunity cost. A book borrowed from the library does not have a monetary cost to the patron but does have an opportunity cost of acquiring and reading it. Watching a television broadcast does not have a monetary cost but does have an opportunity cost.

In any cost-benefit analysis the analyst must be concerned with the opportunity cost of all alternatives to determine the economically efficient management or policy decision. Using only the financial cost for management decisions will result in economic costs being underestimated and may, therefore, lead to decisions that decrease economic efficiency. For example, the cost of a new, remote storage library may be less expensive than that of a new on-campus library for a college or university. However, the economic cost of a remote storage library must include the opportunity cost of time spent by patrons waiting for books to be delivered. Interlibrary loan services, newspaper delivery, college classes, and even information delivery over the Internet have opportunity costs of time spent.

The cost of a journal article includes the financial cost of acquiring it and the opportunity cost of time spent reading it. The opportunity cost of time spent reading a journal article will, typically, be greater than the financial cost of the journal. Consider a journal that has a $5,000 annual subscription price. Assume that this journal is used by research scientists earning $100 per hour. The $100 per hour that their company pays them can be considered the hourly productivity or hourly value to the company of these scientists. If a scientist spends one hour of time to read a journal article, the opportunity cost of the article is $100. If 10 scientists at the company each read an average of five articles from the journal each year, they "spend" $5,000 in time consuming the information in this journal. If the scientists spend this amount of time reading this journal, we can assume that they expect to receive at least $5,000 in value from the journal. The company would like these scientists to receive at least $10,000 in benefit for the journal, that is, the value of the time spent plus the subscription price of the journal.

Another example of an opportunity cost is the value of time spent waiting for information to be delivered. If a research library does not subscribe to a journal, the library will usually acquire articles from that journal for patrons who request the articles through interlibrary loan. Patrons must then wait for delivery. In many libraries patrons can pay for "rush" or "express" delivery of the articles for an extra fee. Assume that the fee is $10. A patron must then make the decision whether the $10 fee is greater than the opportunity cost of waiting a few days for delivery. If the opportunity cost is greater than $10, the patron will pay the $10 for express delivery. If the opportunity cost is less than $10, the patron will wait. A 1996 study of patrons at the University Center Libraries of the State University of New York at Albany, Binghamton, Buffalo, and Stony Brook showed that, on average, the opportunity cost to patrons of waiting for delivery was $2.60.[1] For some patrons, the opportunity cost was much higher. For others, it was lower.

Although the value of time is the most frequently cited example of opportunity cost, the opportunity cost of a decision is more broadly defined as the value of forgone opportunities. Making a choice implies that alternative opportunities are forgone. For example, the opportunity cost of a library lending a book to a patron for six months is the possible value other patrons may have received from that book if they had access to it. The opportunity cost of taking a seat in a popular lecture is the value of that seat to someone else who may not be able to attend if all the seats are filled. In each example, there is limited access to a good or service, and it must be rationed among possible patrons.

Another example of opportunity cost is the "value" of an entrepreneur's time in a company. The cost to the company of its employees is their salaries and benefits. However, the entrepreneur does not receive a salary from his company. Instead, he receives the profit of revenue over costs. The opportunity cost to the owner is the amount of money he could receive if he worked at another company.

Because there is no price or charge associated with opportunity costs, they are more difficult to calculate than financial costs. However, it is important to estimate the opportunity costs of goods and services to make efficient management and policy decisions. It is particularly important to make these estimations for information goods and services where time spent consuming or waiting can be significant.

Other Cost Definitions

Besides the preceding cost definitions, several other important cost definitions are used in cost analysis. These include first-copy costs and overhead costs; indirect and direct costs; accounting, economic, implicit, and explicit costs; sunk costs; and real, nominal, and life-cycle costs.

First-copy and *overhead* costs are fixed costs. First-copy costs refer to the fixed costs of producing a book, journal, or other piece of information before it is reproduced by the publisher for distribution. Overhead costs include the cost of management, administrators, utilities, and other fixed costs that cannot be assigned to an individual unit within the organization. These costs are divided among the units or cost centers within the organization and are therefore sometimes referred to as *allocated* or *indirect* costs. For example, within an academic library the cost of administration, utilities, and value of the building may add a 25 percent overhead cost to all units within the library. *Direct* costs are the costs of a unit or department directly attributable to its goods or services. Salary costs for the employees who work in that unit are direct costs.

Economic costs equal accounting costs plus opportunity or *implicit* costs. *Accounting* costs are *explicit* costs, or the cost of salaries, utilities, the mortgage, and any other cost that must be paid. Economic costs include the implicit costs that are not included in accounting costs. For example, a library fundraiser may cost the library $100 for printing and postage to request donations. However, if volunteers spend their time producing and distributing fliers for the fundraiser, the value or opportunity cost of volunteer time is an economic cost. Within the private sector information industry implicit costs include the value of the company owners' or board of directors' time. For example, a small business owner may have an implicit cost of time of $100,000 per year. This is the salary that the owner could receive if he worked at another firm in the information industry. If at the end of the year the company's profits are $40,000, the owner may feel that this accounting profit is less than his implicit cost of time. The owner may close the company and take a job in the private sector because his economic costs are greater than his revenue.

Sunk costs are expenditures incurred that cannot be changed and, therefore, should not affect current decisions. Sunk costs include the costs of a building already completed, a telecommunications network already finished, or research and development already spent. Sunk costs influence a company's profits but should not influence current decisions. For example, assume that $5 million has been spent on research and development for a new pharmaceutical that has a potential profit of $6 million. Assume that the new drug has not been fully developed or tested. New information indicates that completing the research will cost an additional $2 million. The $5 million in completed research is a sunk cost. Therefore, the additional $2 million should be spent if it is likely that this will complete the research and lead to a potential revenue of $6 million. If the company does not complete the research it will have lost $5 million with no added revenue. However, if it completes the research the company will have spent a total of $7 million to gain $6 in revenue. On net, the company will lose only $1 million by completing the research.

Real or *inflation adjusted* costs are costs adjusted for the rate of inflation. A cost of $10,000 ten years ago is different than a $10,000 cost today. The difference is that $10,000 ten years ago had more purchasing power. Costs can be adjusted for inflation by using the Consumer Price Index or the Producer Price Index. These indexes show how average prices have changed over several years. *Nominal* costs are not adjusted for inflation. *Life-cycle* costs consider the costs of maintenance and depreciation over the life of a purchase. The life-cycle costs of a machine include maintenance and depreciation over the expected life of the machine of 5 or 10 years.

Supply and Costs

Table 2.4 (see p. 16) shows the cost of producing a computer game, but it does not indicate what level of production the producer will choose. The number of CDs a producer is willing to make depends on the market price she believes she can get for each one. In part, this depends on how competitive the producer of computer games believes this market is. In this chapter, the assumption is made that the producer is one of 50 producers of computer software games, a very competitive market. Each producer would like to undercut the price of the competing producers, if possible, to increase market share, and any individual producer may assume that she cannot significantly increase the price of a computer software game without losing consumers to other producers. If one company sells inexpensive software games for $15 and all other companies sell games that are similar in quality and content for $8, most consumers will purchase the $8 games. Therefore, it can be assumed that each producer is a "pricetaker" who accepts the going market price as a price she can charge for an inexpensive computer software game.

Software, Games, Inc., will sell inexpensive computer games as long as the company makes a profit on them. The number of CDs the company will offer on the market is determined by weighing the marginal cost against the market price. If the current market price is $8, Software Games, Inc., expects to receive revenue of $8 for each CD sold. The company will produce and sell CDs until the marginal cost of a disk equals $8. This is illustrated in Table 2.5.

Table 2.5
Software Games, Inc., Profit Schedule

CDs	Total Cost	Average Cost per CD	Marginal Cost per CD	Total Revenue at $8 per CD	Profit
0	$5,000				
500	$6,500	$13.00	$3.00	$4,000	($2,500)
1,000	$7,900	$7.90	$2.80	$8,000	$100
1,500	$9,600	$6.40	$3.40	$12,000	$2,400
2,000	$11,700	$5.85	$4.20	$16,000	$4,300
2,500	$14,300	$5.72	$5.20	$20,000	$5,700
3,000	$17,500	$5.83	$6.40	$24,000	$6,500
3,500	$21,400	$6.11	$7.80	$28,000	$6,600
4,000	$26,100	$6.53	$9.40	$32,000	$5,900

As the number of CDs produced and sold increases, profits increase until somewhere between 3,500 and 4,000 disks. At 3,500 disks the marginal cost is $7.80. At a price of $8, Software Games, Inc., will make $0.20 in profit on each CD made and sold. However, at 4,000 CDs the marginal cost is $9.40. At a price of $8, the company is loosing $1.40 for each disk made and sold. As long as the marginal cost of a CD is less than the price, the company will make a profit from making and selling that disk. Therefore, a producer wanting to maximize profits will make and sell goods and services as long as the marginal cost is less than the price the goods and services can be sold at. This is illustrated in Figure 2.4.

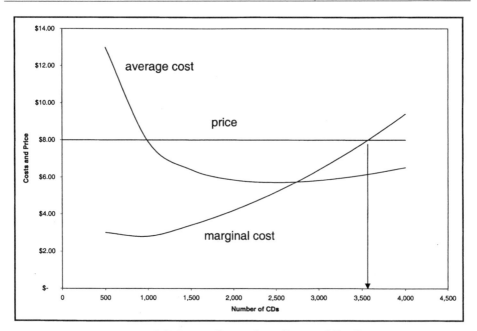

Figure 2.4. Software Games, Inc., Costs and Profits.

Software Games' profits are maximized where the price line in Figure 2.4 crosses the marginal cost line. The profit can be calculated by subtracting the average cost per CD from the price per disk at this level of production, and multiplying this average profit per disk by the number of CDs made and sold. If **Q** is quantity, **AC** is average cost, and **P** is price, then the formula for profit is **Q*(P − AC)**. If **MC** is marginal cost, then profit is maximized at the quantity **Q** such that **P = MC.**

If the market price decreases, then Software Games, Inc., will decrease the variable inputs it employs, thereby decreasing its marginal cost, and produce at a level such that the marginal cost equals the new market price. Remember that Software Games, Inc., has only a single, over-used CD press. If the market price falls, the company will be able to decrease overtime for employees or decrease the number of employees. If the market price increases, the company will try to increase output by hiring more employees (variable inputs) until the marginal cost increases to the new price.

For each new market price, the company is setting output at a level where the marginal cost equals the new price level. Therefore, the company supplies output to the market based on its marginal cost curve. For any given price, the company supply of output is such that the marginal cost equals the price. The marginal cost curve for a company is the company's supply curve.

Market Supply

The market supply curve is the sum of the supply curves for each of the companies producing in this market. If there are 50 firms in the market for inexpensive computer software games and each produces, on average, 3,600 CDs when the market price is $8, then there will be 180,000 CDs supplied to the market. This is illustrated in Figure 2.5.

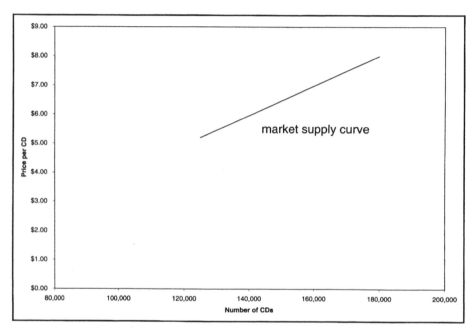

Figure 2.5. Market Supply of Computer Game CDs.

The market supply curve shows how much output will be available in the market at any given price. Locate a price on the vertical axis. The supply curve can be used to estimate how many CDs will be offered in the market at that price. If the market price increases, existing companies will increase production and the number of CDs supplied to the market will increase. Changing the price in a market will change the quantity offered for sale, as shown by the market supply curve.

With 50 companies producing in this market, each company will make approximately one-fiftieth of the total market supply. It is easy to understand how Software Games, Inc., can feel like a price-taker in this competitive market. With this number of firms making similar software games, no single firm has control of or significant influence in the market.

Changes in Market Supply

Changes in the underlying structure of the market will change market supply. For example, if the cost of inputs (e.g., blank CDs, staff wages) increases, company costs for all units of output will increase. Computer game software companies will not be willing to produce the same number of CDs at the new, lower market price. This change in supply is illustrated in Figure 2.6.

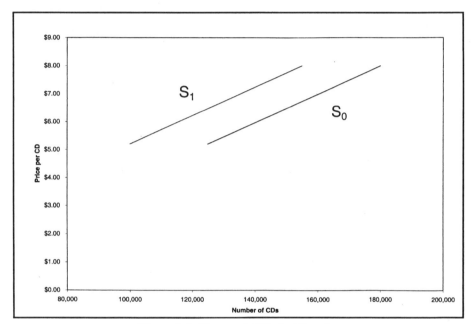

Figure 2.6. Changes in Market Supply.

The increase in the cost of inputs results in a decrease in the supply of CDs from S_0 to S_1. At each price level, fewer CDs are offered for sale in the market. If the price of inputs decreases there will be an increase in supply, illustrated by a shift in the supply curve to the right.

In the same way, when technology changes, the market supply will change. For example, if a new, faster, and less-expensive process for pressing CDs were developed, the supply of CDs would increase at every price.

Price Elasticity of Supply

The slope of a supply curve indicates how responsive output is to changes in price and, therefore, how marginal cost changes as output changes. The price elasticity of supply measures the responsiveness of supply to changes in the market price. The price elasticity of supply is defined as the percentage change in quantity supplied resulting from a 1 percent change in price. This is shown in equation 2.1,

$$\eta = \frac{\delta Q / Q \bullet 100\%}{\delta P / P \bullet 100\%} \qquad (2.1)$$

where δQ is the change in quantity supplied and δP is the change in the market price. The numerator is the percentage change in quantity. The denominator is the percentage change in price. The price elasticity of supply is a number between 0 and infinity. When the price elasticity of supply is greater than 1, supply is elastic, meaning that if the market price increases, producers will increase the supply in the market by a greater percentage. For example, if the price elasticity of supply is 1.6, a 10 percent increase in price will result in a 16 percent increase in supply to the market. When the price elasticity of supply is less than 1, supply is inelastic, in which case there is a limit to the supply that can be made available on the market. If the price elasticity of supply is 0.2, a 10 percent increase in price will result in only a 2 percent increase in output.

Supply is perfectly elastic when a small change in price results in a large change in the quantity supplied. A perfectly elastic supply curve is shown in Figure 2.7, in which a small increase in price results in a large increase in quantity supplied to the market. A small decrease in price results in a large decrease in quantity supplied. In these markets the marginal cost of production is constant and the market has more than one competitive producer.

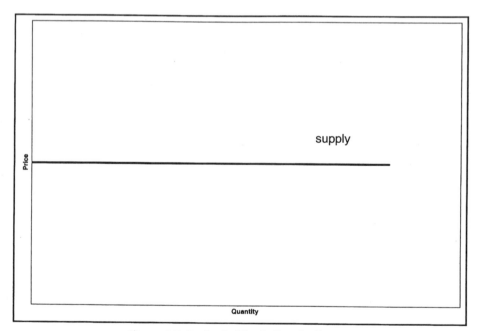

Figure 2.7. Perfectly Elastic Supply Curve.

For example, consider the supply of copier paper. Many companies, both national and local, make and sell copier paper at a price of about $10 per ream of 500 sheets. If one producer were to sell copier paper, of equal quality, at a price of $12 per ream, it would loose business to its competitors. This makes paper suppliers price-takers; each accepts the going market price of $10 per ream. Yet each company is capable of producing a considerable supply of paper as long as sales remain high enough at this price to generate a profit. Each company's cost structure for paper-making will be similar. Given this, it is likely that the market supply curve for paper is perfectly elastic. The supplies of pencils, floppy disks, and paperback romance novels also have perfectly elastic supply curves.

Conversely, in some markets the price elasticity of supply equals 0. A 0 price elasticity of supply is a perfectly inelastic market. In this case, regardless of the increase in price, producers cannot make more of the good or service. For example, the supply of first editions of Oliver Twist by Charles Dickens is fixed regardless of the price. The price may increase or decrease for these rare books, but the quantity of them is fixed. The supply of any rare book, painting, or manuscript is perfectly inelastic. Figure 2.8 shows a perfectly inelastic supply curve.

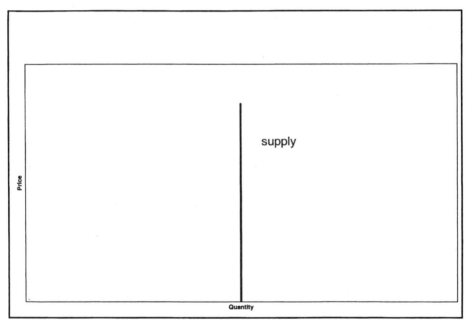

Figure 2.8. Perfectly Inelastic Supply Curve.

Summary

A company's or organization's cost structure determines its supply of goods and services. Supply can be elastic or inelastic depending on the responsiveness of producers to changing quantity in response to changes in price. This responsiveness is determined by the cost of inputs and how rapidly producers can change inputs within the defined time period. Even for organizations that do not supply goods and services for sale to a market, the organization's cost structure determines how rapidly outputs can be increased or decreased.

Costs can be defined as fixed, variable, marginal, average, total, or sunk. The difference between fixed and variable inputs is defined by the chosen period of time. The shorter the time period, the more inputs are defined as fixed instead of variable. Given enough time, all inputs are variable and can be changed.

The cost structure of information goods is different from that of classical economic goods. First, information goods have a significant opportunity cost of consumption. Information delivered in books, magazines, CDs, or television broadcasts requires individuals to spend time to consume it. This time spent consuming information is the opportunity cost of information goods and services. Second, information goods and services frequently have high fixed costs and relatively low marginal costs of reproduction. First-copy, set-up, and research and development costs are all fixed costs of information production. Printing another copy of a book, downloading a copy of a software program, or making a copy of a CD has a much lower cost. The low marginal cost of reproduction influences information pricing, reproduction of information by competitors and consumers, and the types of information delivery. It requires laws to protect intellectual property rights and encourage innovation. This property is explored throughout this book.

Notes

1. See Bruce R. Kingma and Suzanne Irving, *The Economics of Access versus Ownership to Scholarly Information* (Binghamton, NY: Haworth Press, 1996).

Chapter 3

Benefits

Whenever you buy a book, magazine, newspaper, or computer program; make a telephone call; rent a video; or buy a movie ticket, you are expressing your demand for that good or service. The demand for a good or service is the amount of it that consumers are willing and able to purchase in a given period of time. This year, you may buy 10 books, 100 newspapers, 2 computer programs, and 50 hours of long-distance phone calls, and spend 200 hours watching television and 500 hours on the Internet. Your consumption of these goods and services shows your demand for them. The amount you spend in money and time shows your willingness-to-pay for them. This willingness-to-pay for goods and services reflects the benefit you receive from them.

Consumers make decisions about how much of a good or service to purchase based on the price, their level of income, the prices of similar or related goods, and their tastes or preferences for a particular good or service. Consumer theory explains how to quantify or measure these factors to predict how a change in any one factor will influence the quantity demanded. For example, if the price of a long-distance phone call were to increase from $0.05 to $0.10 per minute, you might decrease the amount of time you spend on the phone or decrease the number of long-distance calls you make. In addition, you might disconnect your teenager's telephone and send more e-mail. Each of these decisions is an expression of a change in the quantity of long-distance phone service demanded as a result of a change in the price of long distance. Likewise, if your income were to increase by 20 percent, or if your computer network connection failed for several days, or if you were to move to another state, your demand for long-distance phone service would likely change. Consumer theory helps to predict and measure these changes.

Economists use the demand for goods and services to measure the benefit consumers receive from them. The demand for a good is the amount a consumer is willing to pay for a quantity of the good. Consumer willingness-to-pay can be used to measure the benefit from the good. This is important in determining the benefit or value of goods and services provided by government and nonprofit organizations and in determining the efficiency of markets. Measured benefits can be compared to costs to help analysts and policymakers. Cost-benefit analysis assists policymakers in decisions about building a new library, creating a new data network, or changing copyright laws. In each situation, analysts must measure the benefit consumers or patrons receive from the new library or new data network, or the benefit received in the market by changes in the copyright law.

Demand

The demand for a good or service is the quantity a consumer or consumers are willing to purchase at a given price level. The quantity may be the number of books, floppy disks, newspapers, or computers. It may be the number of gigabits of storage space, square feet of a building, visits to a web site, hours of cellular phone service, or hours of television viewing.

Five factors influence the demand for a good or service: the price of the good, consumer income, the prices of related goods, consumer tastes, and the number of consumers. Of these five factors, the price of the good connects the consumers of the good to the producers. Consumers pay a price that suppliers receive as revenue. The price of a good serves as a mechanism of exchange between demanders and suppliers. The price also provides information to producers and consumers about the benefit consumers receive from a good and the cost to suppliers of producing it.

Price

The relationship between the price of a good and the quantity demanded is expressed in the law of demand. The law of demand is that there is an inverse relationship between the price a consumer pays and the quantity demanded. If the price of a good increases, consumers decrease the amount of it they purchase. If the price decreases, consumers increase the amount of the good they purchase. This law holds for individual consumers as well as the market.

Table 3.1 illustrates the law of demand, showing the results of a simple, hypothetical market survey of two individuals—Patrick and Sabra—who are potential buyers of music CDs. The demand for music CDs by Patrick and Sabra in a year is the number of CDs they are willing to purchase at a given price.

Table 3.1
Individual and Market Annual Demand for Music CDs

Price	Patrick's Demand	Sabra's Demand	All Others	Market Demand
$25	1	0	100,000	100,001
$20	2	0	120,000	120,002
$15	3	2	140,000	140,005
$10	4	4	160,000	160,008
$5	5	7	180,000	180,012

According to Table 3.1, if the average price of a CD is $25, Patrick will purchase one CD a year but Sabra will not purchase a CD. If the price of a CD falls to $15, Patrick will purchase 3 CDs and Sabra will purchase 2. Both Patrick and Sabra increase their CD purchases as the price falls.

The market demand for a good is the sum of the individual demand by each consumer. As the price falls from $20 to $15, annual sales increase from 120,002 to 140,005 CDs. The increase in market demand is the sum of the increase in purchases by existing consumers plus additional purchases by new consumers. Patrick increases his purchases from two to three, and Sabra enters the market as a new consumer. Figure 3.1 shows the relationship between price and quantity demanded using the information in Table 3.1.

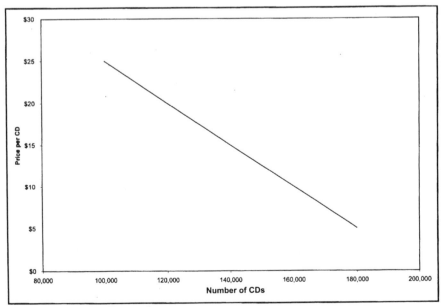

Figure 3.1. Market Demand.

Patrick's purchases, as part of the market demand, can be identified in Figure 3.1. The first CD Patrick buys is the 100,001st CD sold in the market. The second CD Patrick buys is the 120,002nd CD sold. Each individual CD is purchased by a single consumer and is a single point on the demand curve in Figure 3.1.

Changes in Demand

Although the price of a good or service influences the quantity consumers demand, other factors also influence demand. Changes in consumer income, prices of related goods, tastes, and the number of consumers can change the demand for a good or service. Economists focus on measurable factors that influence demand because the effects on demand can be quantified; however, many things may influence how consumers behave.

For most goods and services, as income increases, the demand for that good or service increases. If income increases, consumers may purchase more CDs or books, rent more videos, or use the extra income to purchase more of other goods and services. If the quantity demanded of a good increases when consumer income increases, it is called a *normal* good.

Returning to the example in Table 3.1, assume Sabra was earning $30,000 a year. If Sabra's income increases to $35,000 a year, she may increase the quantity of CDs she purchases, at any price level. Her demand curve will shift to the right. This is shown in Table 3.2 and Figure 3.2. In Figure 3.2, as her income increases, her demand shifts from D_0 to D_1.

Table 3.2 Effect of Increase in Income on Sabra's Demand		
Price	Sabra's Demand ($30,000 salary)	Sabra's Demand ($35,000 salary)
$25	0	0
$20	0	2
$15	2	4
$10	4	6
$5	7	9

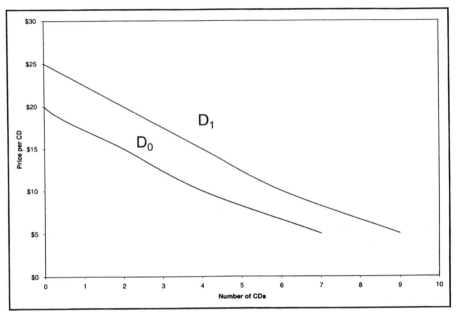

Figure 3.2. Income Effect.

For some goods and services, an increase in consumer income will decrease the demand. These goods are called *inferior* goods. Typically, consumers at a higher level of income will purchase the higher quality equivalent of the good. Examples of goods that may, for some consumers, be inferior goods are paperback books, classes at a community college, or computers with the Pentium Celeron™ processor. For each good there is another good—hardcover books, university classes, a Pentium III™ processor—that consumers might consider to be of higher quality. If consumer income increases, some consumers decrease their purchases of the inferior goods.

If prices of related goods change, consumer demand might also change. There are two categories of related goods: substitutes and complements. *Substitute* goods are goods where an increase in the price of one good will cause the demand for the other good to increase. Consumers view the two goods as substitutes. If a consumer does not purchase one of the goods, he may instead purchase the other. Music CDs and music cassette tapes are substitutes. If the price of the CD is too high, a consumer may purchase the cassette instead. Other examples of substitute goods are VCR and DVD players, paperback and hardcover books, and print and online newspapers. If the price of one good increases, the demand for the other good will increase, and as the price of the good decreases, the demand for the other good will decrease.

Information can be delivered in a variety of formats. The different delivery formats are substitute goods. Video and DVD, cassettes and CDs, CD-ROMs and floppy disks, print and online, hardcover and paperback, journals and books can all be substitute goods. Consumers are more interested in the information than the format; however, different formats are not perfect substitutes for each other. Many consumers are only interested in renting a movie on video because they do not have a DVD player. Even if the price of renting a video increases, these consumers will not rent the movie on DVD.

Complementary goods and services are those for which a decrease in the price will increase the quantity purchased of the other good. For example, video rentals and video cassette recorders are complementary goods. If the price of VCRs were to decrease there might be an increase in the number of videos rented. The lower price on VCRs will increase the number of VCRs purchased and, likewise, may increase the number of videos rented. This effect is shown in Figures 3.3 and 3.4. In Figure 3.3, the price of a VCR at a local store has decreased from $225 to $200. As a result, the number of VCRs purchased in the community increased from 1,100 to 1,200 a month. As a result of that increase, the demand for videotapes rented at video stores has increased from demand curve D_0 to D_1. If the price of a video rental is $3.50, the video stores would see an increase in rentals from 60,000 to 65,000 a month.

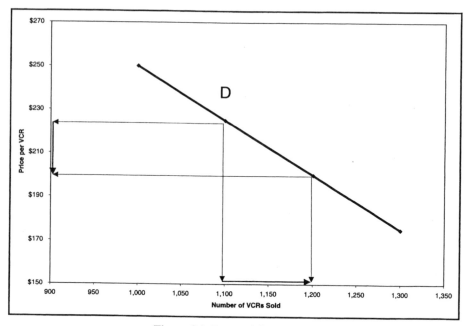

Figure 3.3. Demand for VCRs.

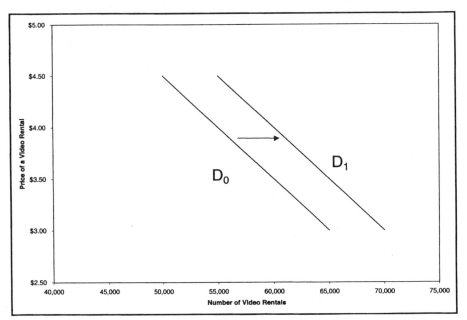

Figure 3.4. Effect on Demand for Video Rentals.

Information goods sometimes depend on technology to deliver access. The technology and the sale of the good or service are likely to be complementary goods. DVD players and DVD disk rentals, computers and floppy disks, CD players and CDs, video game players and video games, are all complementary goods. Other examples of complementary goods are college classes and college textbooks, paper and pencils, and reading glasses and books. As the price of one good increases the demand for the other good may decrease, and as the price decreases the demand for the other good may increase.

The number of consumers, consumer tastes and preferences, and other factors can influence demand. Because the market demand is the sum of individual demand, if the number of consumers increases, the demand for a good increases and the demand curve shifts to the right. Sometimes a good will be fashionable or a fad, temporarily increasing demand for the good. Goods can also go out of fashion, resulting in a decrease in demand. Finally, other factors may increase consumer tastes for a good and increase the demand for a good. A television broadcast about World War II might increase the demand for books and videos on World War II. A news story about food poisoning at a popular restaurant might decrease the restaurant demand, shifting the demand curve to the left.

Price Elasticity of Demand

The influence of price on the quantity demand is measured by the price elasticity of demand. The price elasticity of demand enables economists to quantify the effect or price on the quantity demanded. Using data on price and quantity demand, we can measure the price elasticity of demand. If the price changes, the price elasticity of demand can be used to measure the likely change in quantity demanded.

The formula for the price elasticity of demand is shown in equation 3.1,

$$\varepsilon = \frac{\delta Q / Q \bullet 100\%}{\delta P / P \bullet 100\%} \tag{3.1}$$

where δQ is the change in quantity demanded and δP is the change in the market price. The numerator is the percentage change in quantity. The denominator is the percentage change in price. The price elasticity of demand is the percentage change in the quantity demanded divided by the percentage change in the price. A 10 percent increase in price that results in a 5 percent decrease in the quantity demanded will have a price elasticity of 0.5. A 10 percent decrease in price that results in a 25 percent increase in the quantity demanded will have a price elasticity of 2.5. The price elasticity is a negative number, because the price and quantity always change in opposite directions; however, it is frequently represented by a positive number with the implicit assumption that when price increases, quantity decreases.

A price elasticity of 0.9 means that a 10 percent increase in the price will result in a 9 percent decrease in quantity. A price elasticity of 3.54 means that a 1 percent decrease in the price will result in a 3.54 percent increase in quantity demanded. Table 3.3 shows the calculated price elasticity of demand for cellular phone calls, using hypothetical data from a cellular phone company's records of customer calls.

Table 3.3
Price Elasticity of Demand for Cellular Phone Calls

Price	Percentage Change in Price	Average Minutes of Calls per Month	Percentage Change in Calls	Price Elasticity of Demand
$0.54		10		
	9.6		66.7	6.9
$0.50		20		
	10.5		18.2	1.7
$0.45		24		
	14.3		15.4	1.1
$0.39		28		
	26.1		25.0	1.0
$0.30		36		
	3.4		2.7	0.8
$0.29		37		

As the price per minute of cellular phone calls decreases, the average number of minutes used per month increases. The second column in Table 3.3 shows the percentage change in price using the average price from the first column as the denominator for the calculation. The fourth column shows the percentage change in the quantity. The final column shows the price elasticity of demand.

The price elasticity of demand varies for the same good or service as the price changes. In Table 3.3, as the price decreases the price elasticity of demand decreases. At a high price, the price elasticity will be a higher number. This is because the high price results in a low quantity purchased. Decreasing the price a small percentage will likely increase quantity sold by a larger percentage. At a low price, the price elasticity will be a lower number. At a low price there is likely to be a high quantity demanded of the good. Increasing the price will likely decrease quantity sold by a smaller percentage.

Demand is elastic when the price elasticity of demand is greater than 1. Demand is inelastic when the price elasticity of demand is less than 1. If the price elasticity of demand equals 0, demand is perfectly inelastic. If the price elasticity of demand equals 1, demand is unit-elastic. An elastic price elasticity of demand means that consumers are very responsive to changes in price. An inelastic price elasticity of demand means that consumers are unresponsive; that is, they will continue to purchase about the same quantity of the good regardless of the price increase or decrease. Perfectly elastic and inelastic demand curves are shown in Figures 3.5 and 3.6.

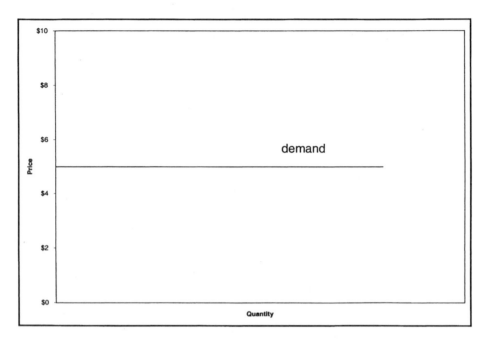

Figure 3.5. Perfectly Elastic Demand.

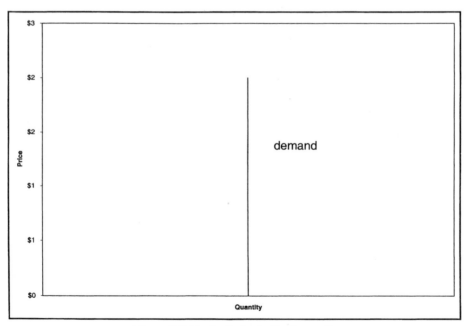

Figure 3.6. Perfectly Inelastic Demand.

In Figure 3.5, a small increase in the price will result in quantity demanded falling to 0. A small decease in the price will result in quantity demanded increasing significantly. Consumers show a dramatic response to changes in price. In Figure 3.6, an increase or decrease in price has little effect on consumer demand. Price has little influence on the quantity of consumer demand. Table 3.4 provides several examples of goods and services with elastic and inelastic demand.

Table 3.4 Elastic and Inelastic Demand	
Goods and Services with Elastic Demand	**Goods and Services with Inelastic Demand**
Photocopies from one of 10 photocopy machines at the library	Drugs manufactured and patented as the only cure for a terminal disease
Inexpensive radios from one of many radio manufacturers	Subscriptions to the top scholarly science journal title
Copies of a single title from a collection of paperback romance novels	Correct and complete information on the status of nuclear weapons development by foreign countries
Floppy disks sold by one of many companies	Services of a knowledgeable and competent surgeon for completing heart transplants
Stock trades at one online stock broker company	Services of a top antitrust lawyer who successfully defends clients against antitrust law suits
Books from one online book distributor	

Elastic goods have close substitutes that provide a similar good or service. Amazon.com cannot sell a book at a price significantly above the price charged by barnesandnoble.com, or customers will purchase it from the competition. Inelastic goods are necessities for which there are few substitutes. If a patient has a potentially terminal disease, the patient wants the drug that cures him and is willing to pay for it regardless of the price. University research libraries must have the top scientific journals for their patrons. As a result, the demand for the top science journals is inelastic.

For obvious reasons, producers would rather sell in markets with inelastic demand for their goods than with elastic demand. An inelastic demand curve allows the seller to increase price and profits without significantly decreasing the quantity sold. This is the reason suppliers advertise in an effort to build brand awareness among consumers. If consumers must have a certain product brand that they believe is of higher quality, the demand for that brand will have a more inelastic demand curve. Information about the brand and its qualities can change the elasticity of demand.

Several economists have estimated the price elasticity of demand for information goods and services. Bebensee, Strauch, and Strauch and Chressanthis and Chressanthis show an inelastic demand for journal subscriptions by academic libraries.[1] Woolsey and Strach and Chressanthis and Chressanthis show how an inelastic demand enables foreign publishers to pass exchange rate risk on to libraries in the United States.[2] Kingma demonstrates that university library photocopying has an inelastic demand.[3] Lankford illustrates an inelastic demand by parents for elementary and secondary school education for their children.[4] In a classic paper on econometric estimation of information demand, Daly and Mayor demonstrate that the demand for telephone calls to directory assistance was a very inelastic 0.15,[5] and Crandall shows elastic demand for basic cable television service of 2.2.[6]

Consumer Surplus

The demand for a good is used not only to determine how much of a good will be purchased at a given price but also to quantify the value or benefit a consumer derives from his or her purchase. This benefit is called consumer surplus, and it can be quantified by using the consumer willingness-to-pay for a good as an estimate of the benefit a consumer receives from the good.

We can use the example of the demand for CDs to show this. In Table 3.1, if a CD costs $25, Patrick is willing to purchase one CD. If Patrick's benefit from a CD was less than $25, he would not have purchased it. If Patrick's benefit was more than $25, he would have purchased it at a higher price and would be willing to purchase more than one CD at $25. Therefore, Patrick's benefit from the first CD he purchases is $25.

If the price decreases to $20 per CD, Patrick is willing to purchase a second CD. Patrick's willingness to pay for the second CD is $20 and, therefore, his benefit from the second CD is $20. This is Patrick's marginal willingness-to-pay or marginal benefit for the second CD. If Patrick purchases two CDs, he will receive a marginal benefit of $25 from the first and $20 from the second. His total benefit from two CDs is $45.

If CDs cost $20 each, Patrick will purchase two. This is because the marginal benefit from the first CD is greater than the price, and the marginal benefit from the second CD equals the price. The marginal benefit from the third CD is only $15, so Patrick will not purchase it. Patrick pays $40 for $45 in benefit. The difference between the benefit Patrick receives and the amount paid is his consumer surplus.

At a lower price, Patrick purchases more CDs, receiving more benefit from CDs and more consumer surplus. At a price of $15 per CD, Patrick purchases three CDs, receives a total benefit of $60, pays $45, and receives a consumer surplus of $15. This is illustrated by the demand curve **D** shown in Figure 3.7.

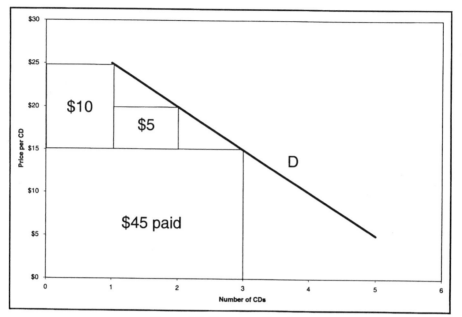

Figure 3.7. Consumer Surplus.

The consumer surplus is $10 from the first CD, $5 from the second, and $0 from the third. The amount paid is a rectangle with a height equal to the price and a length equal to the number of CDs purchased.

As the price of CDs decreases, Patrick's consumer surplus increases. Suppose CDs go on sale for $5 each. Patrick purchases five CDs and receives a benefit from each CD of $25, $20, $15, $10, and $5. Patrick's total benefit from CDs is $75. He pays $5 per CD for a total of $25. His consumer surplus is $50. The increase in consumer surplus comes from the lower price he pays on the first three CDs and the additional purchase of two CDs. The price per CD decreases from $15 to $5, a $10 savings on the first three CDs Patrick would have purchased even at the higher price. This is a $30 increase in consumer surplus. In addition, Patrick purchases two more CDs with a marginal benefit of $10 and $5 each. The $5 price results in an additional $5 in consumer surplus from the fourth CD purchased. Consumer surplus increases by $35 from $15, at a price of $15 per CD, to $50, at a price of $5 per CD. This is shown in Figure 3.8.

This same effect happens in the market for CDs. Consumer surplus is the difference between the benefit consumers receive from goods and the amount paid for the goods. It is the sum of consumer surplus to individual consumers like Patrick. As the price decreases in the market, the consumer surplus will increase. This is demonstrated in the market for CDs in Figure 3.9.

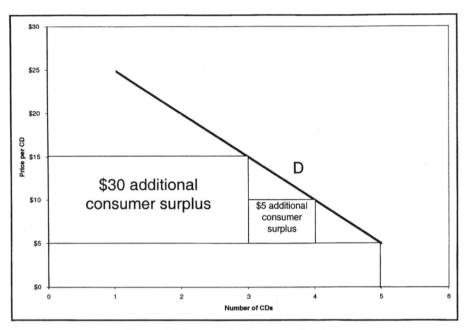

Figure 3.8. Increase in Consumer Surplus.

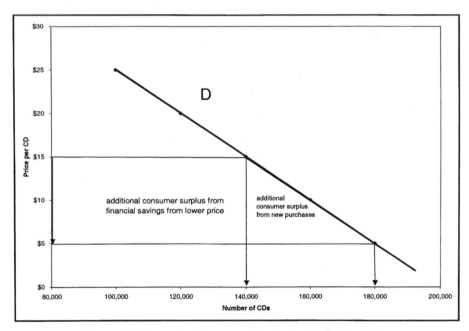

Figure 3.9. Change in Consumer Surplus in Market for CDs.

Figure 3.9 shows the increase in consumer surplus in the market for CDs resulting from the price decrease of $15 to $5 per CD and the quantity increase of 140,000 to 180,000 CDs. The price decrease results in financial savings for consumers. The financial savings equals the $10 savings multiplied by 140,000 CDs, the number of CDs that would have been purchased even at the higher price. The consumer surplus resulting from financial savings equals $1,400,000. Consumer surplus also increases from the increase in quantity demanded. This consumer surplus equals the triangle in Figure 3.9, which equals one-half of $10 multiplied by the additional 40,000 CDs. The increase in consumer surplus coming from an increase in quantity equals $200,000. The total increase in consumer surplus equals $1,600,000.

Summary

Economists measure the benefit of goods and services by consumer demand. The consumer demand is influenced by the price of the good, prices of related goods, income, tastes, and other factors. The price of the good reflects consumer willingness-to-pay for the good or the consumers' measure of the benefit they believe they will receive from it. Consumer surplus is the net benefit or benefit minus the amount paid for goods and services.

With information goods and services, calculating the benefits received can be difficult. The benefit from information is not received until after it is consumed and paid for. Once consumed, it cannot typically be returned. Once a book is read, you cannot return the information. However, you cannot judge the value of the book without reading it. In spite of these issues, economists use the demand for books, magazines, newspapers, and other forms of information to measure a consumer's expected benefit from the information. The expected benefit is the value the consumer believes the information has to her prior to consuming it. The actual benefit may be higher, or lower, than the expected benefit; however, the expected benefit is what consumers are willing to pay for it.

Notes

1. Mark Bebensee, Bruce Strauch, and Katina Strauch, "Elasticity and Journal Pricing," *The Acquisitions Librarian* (1989): 219-28; George A. Chressanthis and June D. Chressanthis, "Publisher Monopoly Power and Third-Degree Price Discrimination of Scholarly Journals," *Technical Services Quarterly* (1993): 13-36.

2. W. William Woolsey and A. Bruce Strauch, "The Impact of U.S. Dollar Depreciation on the Prices of Foreign Academic Journals: A Supply and Demand Analysis," *Publishing Research Quarterly* (1992):74-81; George A. Chressanthis and June D. Chressanthis, "A General Econometric Model of he Determinants of Library Subscription Prices and Scholarly Journals: The Role of Exchange Rate Risk and Other Factors," *The Library Quarterly* 64 (1994): 270-93.

3. Bruce R. Kingma, "The Demand for Photocopies and Journal Subscriptions: An Empirical Test of the Librarians' Solution to Journal Pricing," unpublished manuscript, School of Information Science and Policy, University at Albany, 1994.

4. Hamilton Lankford, "Preferences of Citizens for Public Expenditures on Elementary and Secondary Education," *Journal of Econometrics* (1985): 1-20.

5. George Daly and Thomas Major, "Estimating the Value of a Missing Market: The Econometrics of Directory Assistance," *Journal of Law and Economics* (1980): 147-66.

6. R. W. Crandall, "Elasticity of Demand for Cable Service and the Effect of Broadcast Signals on Cable Prices," Appended to TCI Reply Comments in FCC Mass Media Docket, 1990.

Chapter 4

Markets

In 1776, Adam Smith in *The Wealth of Nations* described the market as a place where consumers and producers come together to buy and sell, changing prices and output until an equilibrium market price and market level of output are determined. The "law of the invisible hand" says that within a market consumers and producers bargain over the price of a good, ultimately settling on an equilibrium price. If the price is too high, producers will have a surplus and be forced to lower their price. If the price is too low, shortages will result and consumers will bid up the price. In the end, the "invisible hand" pushes the market price to its equilibrium, eliminating shortages or surpluses. In the end, the equilibrium market price of a newspaper is $0.50, a new book is $40, and a video rental is $3.50.

The price is an allocation mechanism for goods and services. Only efficient producers that have a cost per unit below the price can survive in the market. The price determines which producers remain in the market and which producers do not. Only consumers that have a benefit above the price are willing to purchase the good. Consumers with a benefit below the price will not buy the good. The price determines which producers and which consumers will participate in the market. Price allocates production to sellers who can make a profit. It also allocates consumption to consumers who have the highest value of the good.

For many goods and services there is no market or price. Library services, government information services, and television broadcasts often do not have a financial price that consumers pay or producers receive. However, there is still a demand or benefit from consuming a good or service and a cost from producing it. For these goods, policymakers or managers must sometimes estimate the demand for the good to determine the benefit from the good and estimate the cost of producing the good to make economically efficient decisions about supply and allocation in the absence of a market. How to estimate the benefit and cost of a good without a market is demonstrated at the end of this chapter and in subsequent chapters.

The Market Equilibrium

The market equilibrium is a price and quantity that consumers are willing to pay to purchase the amount producers are willing to supply at a particular price. The market combines consumer demand with producer supply of a good. The market demand and supply for paperback romance novels sold in grocery stores is illustrated in Figure 4.1. Figure 4.1 represents the monthly demand and supply for romance novel books. There may be many book titles represented in Figure 4.1; however, we are modeling the number of books sold in this category regardless of title.

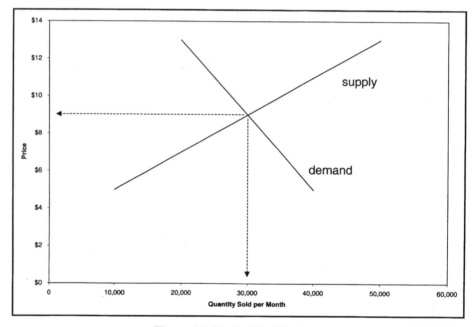

Figure 4.1. Market Equilibrium.

As shown in Figure 4.1, the market equilibrium price for romance novels is $9 and the equilibrium quantity is 30,000 books sold per month. This is an equilibrium price, meaning that the market would push any other price toward the equilibrium of $9. Prices higher than $9 would be pushed lower. Prices lower than $9 would be pushed higher. For example, consider a price of $11. At this price consumers would demand fewer books. According to Figure 4.1, the demand for books would be 25,000 a month. At a price of $11, suppliers would be willing to produce, distribute, and sell more books. At this price the supply of books would be 40,000 a month. The excess inventory of books in stores would result in a sale on romance novels, lowering the price to the original equilibrium of $9. Consider a price of $7. At this lower price, consumers would be willing to purchase more books. According to Figure 4.1, consumers would demand 35,000 books a month. However, at this low price suppliers would only be willing to produce, distribute, and sell 25,000 books a month. As a result, there would be a shortage of 15,000 books a month. The excess consumer demand would result in prices increasing until the market reaches the equilibrium price of $9 a book. The price increase would decrease the quantity consumers demand and increase the quantity producers supply until the market reaches the equilibrium quantity of 30,000 books.

Adam Smith referred to this effect as the "law of the invisible hand." If prices are too low, excess demand will result in consumers bidding prices up. This price increase will induce producers to work overtime, purchase more supplies, and keep factories open longer hours to increase supply. If prices are too high, there will be excess supply. Suppliers will be forced to put this unsold inventory on sale, thereby lowering prices. Lower prices will increase the quantity consumers demand, until price and quantity reach their equilibrium.

Changes in Demand and Supply

As the market demand or supply changes, the resulting change in the market equilibrium will be determined by the elasticity of demand and supply. Figure 4.2 shows the effect of an increase in demand from D_0 to D_1 in the market for paperback romance novels, a product with an elastic supply curves. Supply is elastic because additional titles and books can be produced without a significant increase in the cost per book. Authors of these novels can be hired at a lower cost than more famous authors. Additional paperback books can be produced at a lower cost than hardcover books. Demand may increase for any number of reasons. For example, the grocery stores may have lowered prices on food, thereby increasing the number of consumers in the store and increasing the number of consumers purchasing paperback romance novels.

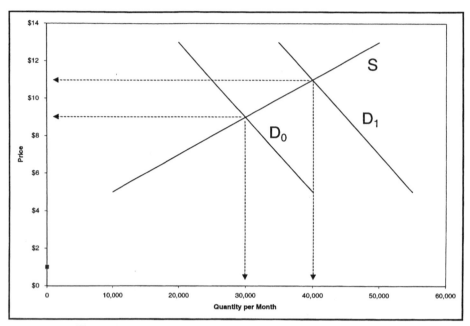

Figure 4.2. Market Equilibrium Changes with Elastic Supply.

Figure 4.2 illustrates the increase in demand and subsequent increase in the equilibrium price to $11 per book and quantity to 40,000 books per month. The elastic supply curve means that there is only a $2 increase in price (22 percent) but a 10,000-book increase in quantity (33 percent). Although prices increase, the percentage increase in price is lower than the percentage increase in quantity. The market for paperback romance novels sold in grocery stores is a highly competitive market, with many publishers producing several inexpensive titles for sale. Any increase in demand can produce an increase in quantity with a smaller effect on price. This occurs with any market in which the supply is elastic. If manufacturers can readily increase or decrease production, then any changes in demand will result in quantity changing more than price.

When supply is inelastic, an increase in demand produces a larger increase in price with a smaller increase in quantity. For example, consider the market for original Altair computers. Although these computers are inferior to current PCs, there is a nostalgic collectors' value to them. In addition, the Altair is not produced anymore. The market for original Altair computers is shown in Figure 4.3.

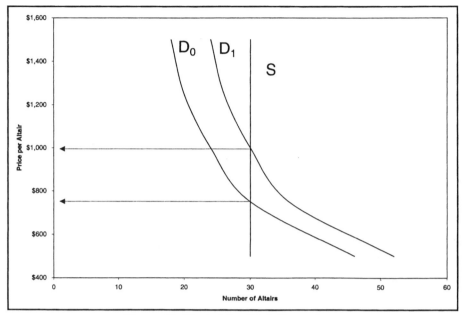

Figure 4.3. Market for Altair Computers.

If there are only 30 Altair computers still in existence, then regardless of the price or demand, there is an inelastic supply. If demand for these antiques equals D_0, then the equilibrium price will be $750 for each computer. If demand increases to D_1, then the equilibrium price will increase to $1,000. The equilibrium quantity cannot increase because Altairs are no longer manufactured. The market for antiques and collectibles can be very volatile, subject to large increases and decreases in price. With changes in demand, the inelastic supply means that quantity cannot change and, therefore, the price must adjust to bring the market back to equilibrium.

Changes in supply will also affect the equilibrium quantity and price. The elasticity of demand determines how changes in supply influence the equilibrium. If demand is elastic, consumers are very responsive to changes in price, and any change in supply will produce a small change in price and a large change in quantity demanded. Consider the market for blank video cassette tapes for home recording made by a particular manufacturer such as the Sony Corporation and sold at a local store. There are many manufacturers of blank videotapes which, to the typical consumer, are nearly indistinguishable from each other. There are also many stores that sell blank videotapes. These factors mean that there will be an elastic demand for the blank Sony tapes at this store. This is illustrated in Figure 4.4.

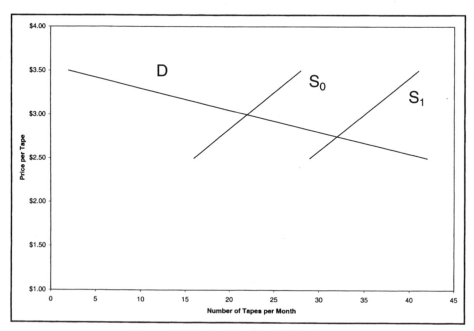

Figure 4.4. Market for Blank Videotapes.

In Figure 4.4, the supply of blank videotapes increases from S_0 to S_1. **D** is the demand for videotapes. This may be the result of a change in technology at this manufacturer that lowers the cost of producing videotapes. With an elastic demand curve, even a slight decrease in the price of blank videotapes will result in a significant increase in the quantity sold. In Figure 4.4, the equilibrium price decreases from $3.00 per tape to $2.75 per tape. The equilibrium quantity demanded increases from 22 tapes to 32 tapes per month. Goods with elastic demand that have many substitutes experience significant shifts in the quantity sold resulting from small changes in price.

When goods have an inelastic demand, changes in supply result in significant changes in the market price with little or no change in the quantity. Consider the demand for urgent or emergency care from your doctor. When you arrive at the emergency room or doctor's office the price of the care is unlikely to affect your decision to request treatment. This is demonstrated in Figure 4.5.

In Figure 4.5, the cost of emergency room services increases, decreasing supply from S_0 to S_1. **D** is the monthly demand for services. The equilibrium price increases from $90 to $120 per visit. However, given the inelastic demand for this service, it is unlikely that there will be a significant decline in the number of patients in the emergency room. In this case, price has little effect on the demand for the service. Other factors, such as the presence of a community health clinic, availability of non-emergency care, time spent waiting in the emergency room for care, and education about treatment of illness, may have an effect on demand.

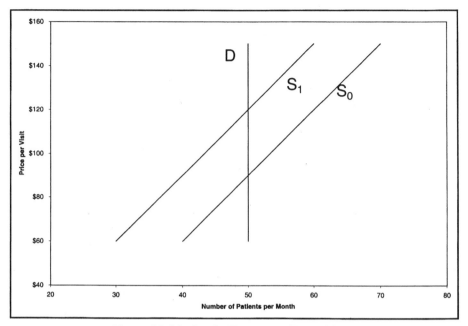

Figure 4.5. Market for Emergency Room Visits.

Information that provides knowledge of alternative goods and services or educates about the value of goods and services can influence the elasticity of demand. Knowledge of alternative goods will make demand more elastic. Knowledge about the high quality of a good or convincing advertising will make the demand for that good less elastic.

Economic Efficiency

The market equilibrium price determines which suppliers and consumers remain in the market. Only suppliers that can produce at a cost below the price will produce and sell in the market. Only consumers that get a benefit greater than the price will purchase the good or service. The market price allocates the production and consumption of the good. The market demand and supply determine the equilibrium market price.

As demonstrated in Chapters 2 and 3, the demand and supply also measure the benefit received from and cost of producing a good. Measuring benefit and cost in a market enables economists to measure the efficiency of a market. A market that is economically efficient is one in which benefits are greater than costs and the difference between benefits and costs is as large as possible.

In Figure 4.6, as output increases, total benefit and total cost increases. As more is produced, costs increase at an increasing rate. As more is consumed, benefits increase at a decreasing rate. The market is at maximum economic efficiency when the net benefit or benefit minus the cost is at a maximum. This is what economists refer to as the *pareto optimum.*

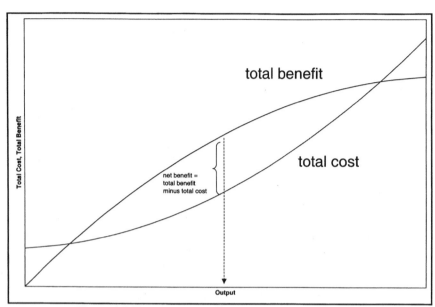

Figure 4.6. Economically Efficient Allocation of a Good.

Under certain conditions, markets will reach this level of output. Under these conditions the competitive market equilibrium price efficiently allocates consumption and production, thereby enabling the market to reach the pareto optimum. This is illustrated in Figure 4.7.

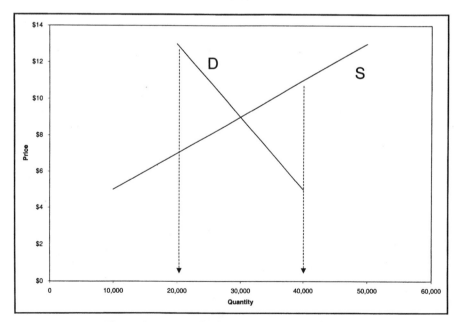

Figure 4.7. Pareto Optimum Market Equilibrium.

In Figure 4.7, the market equilibrium is at a price of $9 and quantity of 30,000. This is the level of output that maximizes social efficiency or net benefit in the market. The level of benefit is measured by consumer willingness-to-pay for this good, or the area under the demand curve. The cost is measured by the marginal cost to producers, or the area under the supply curve. An output of 30,000 maximizes the difference between benefit and cost.

Consider a level of output of 40,000. At this level the marginal cost of the 40,000th unit—as measured by the supply curve—is $11, while the marginal benefit—as measured by the demand curve—is $5. A producer will supply this unit of this good only if the price is at least $11. A consumer will purchase this unit of this good only if the price is no higher than $5. However, it is inefficient for the market to consume a unit of output that provides only $5 in benefit at a cost of $11. Therefore, fewer than 40,000 units should be produced. In fact, for all levels of output greater than 30,000, the marginal cost is greater than the marginal benefit.

At levels of output less than 30,000 the marginal cost is less than the marginal benefit. The 20,000th unit of output has a cost of $7 to a producer and a benefit of $13 to a consumer. This unit of output provides $6 in net benefit to society. If this unit is sold at a price of $9, the consumer receives $4 in consumer surplus ($13 in benefit minus the $9 price) and the producer receives a $2 profit ($9 price minus the $7 cost). Therefore, the 20,000th unit should be supplied by the producer and consumed by the consumer represented in Figure 4.7. The 20,000th unit of output, and all other units less than 30,000 that have a positive net benefit, should be produced and consumed. These units provide consumer surplus to consumers and profit to producers.

The competitive market equilibrium level of output is also the socially efficient level. In Figure 4.7, only those consumers that receive a benefit greater than the equilibrium price of $9 purchase the good. Only suppliers that can produce the good at a cost less than the equilibrium price of $9 produce it. The equilibrium, with consumers and producers acting independently of one another, results in the pareto optimum level of output.

Market Failure

When there are costs or benefits in a market that are not represented in the demand and supply curves, or when the market is prevented from reaching the competitive market equilibrium, there is a market failure. A market failure occurs when the socially efficient or pareto optimum level of output is different from the competitive market equilibrium. An overproduction or underproduction of the good or service may be the result of consumers or producers not taking the external costs or benefits of their actions into account, the lack of a competitive market, or government policies that prevent the market from achieving the socially efficient level of output.

The most obvious and frequently cited example of a market failure is when the production of a good causes pollution. For example, sulfur dioxide and other chemicals are released into the air during the process of making a gallon of paint. This pollution imposes costs on society that are not considered by the producer as part of the firm's costs of production. The manufacturer of paint considers only the costs of supplies, chemicals, and workers used in making paint. Similarly, consumers of paint typically do not consider the pollution caused by the production of paint when they are purchasing it. As a result, the market supply and demand for paint does not incorporate the external costs of the pollution produced during the manufacturing process. The result is a market failure.

Pollution is not the only example of market failure. Whenever costs or benefits are not fully realized or borne by producers and consumers, there is a possibility that the competitive market equilibrium will differ from the pareto optimum. The adverse effects of false advertising that misrepresents a product's quality, negative gossip or lies that damage someone's reputation, false testimony that convicts an innocent person, junk mail that congests mailboxes and wastes your time, and computer viruses that damage computer systems are all examples of costs that are not fully realized by the producer or consumer in these markets. In each case the good should not have been produced, or the output produced in the market will be higher than the socially desired level.

Conversely, when all the benefits of a market are not realized by consumers or producers, when the market is controlled by a single supplier, or when government regulation restricts output, the equilibrium level of output may be less than the pareto optimum. For example, when monopolies in computer software, computer operating systems, or telecommunications result in inflated prices that are significantly above the cost of production, the result is fewer copies sold of software or new operating systems, or less use of telephone services, than is economically efficient. When government regulations and testing prevent the use of new, possibly life-saving pharmaceuticals, there is less output in the market than is socially efficient. However, when the lack of government regulations enables pharmaceutical companies to misrepresent the dangers or value of their drugs, consumers will purchase drugs that do not provide the benefit they are expecting and the level of output in the market will be greater than the socially efficient level.

If consumers do not have full information on the value of a good, they may not purchase it because of the risk of receiving a low quality good. Similarly, insurance providers may not insure worthy clients because they cannot determine the client's level of risk. As a result, the level of output or insurance in the market is less than the socially efficient level.

Information goods and services can sometimes be overproduced and sometimes be underproduced as a result of market failures. Information goods and services can also be produced to correct for market failures. Consumer magazines that report on the quality of goods; information on the quality of health care; news about the quality of government representatives; and health information about the dangers of drugs, tobacco, or alcohol are all examples of information markets that correct market failures elsewhere. Information markets exist to reduce uncertainty and risk in purchasing, health care, legal services, and elsewhere. In these examples economic efficiency is improved.

There are four categories of market failure: (1) externalities, (2) public goods, (3) monopolies, and (4) market failure resulting from consumers or producers not having perfect information about the quality of goods or services. Each type of market failure and its application to the economics of information is discussed in the following chapters. In addition, information markets that result in corrections to these market failures are examined. Each market failure creates the opportunity for another information market to form to correct the problems that exist in the original market.

Summary

The point of intersection of the demand and supply curves determines the market equilibrium price and quantity. The market equilibrium price allocates the production of a good to the suppliers who are the most cost-efficient and consumption of that good to the consumers who derive the most benefit or consumer surplus from their purchase. In the absence of market failure, this equilibrium will result in a pareto optimum, or socially efficient level of output. However, when market failures occur, the level of output in the market will be different than the socially efficient level.

Frequently, the markets for information goods and services suffer from market failure. Unlike other goods, information can be shared, jointly consumed, and provide benefits or costs to those who are not direct consumers or producers; information services can result in monopolies; and the lack of full information can result in uncertainty about the quality of goods and services. These market failures result in an equilibrium level of information goods and services that is different from the pareto optimum level.

The existence of market failure also creates a market for information goods and services that correct the market. Information that reduces uncertainty will move markets closer to their socially efficient level of output.

Sometimes information markets do not correct the market failure, and it is necessary for government intervention to reduce market failure. For example, public education may be a government response to consumers not receiving sufficient education in the free market. Without public education, many children would not receive an education, and subsequently the country would not have a workforce with sufficient education to maintain the country's productivity. Government regulations on truthful advertising are necessary to maintain consumer trust in products and prevent consumers from purchasing potentially dangerous products. The conditions under which government regulations are needed are examined in subsequent chapters.

Chapter 5

Information as a Public Good

Goods consumed by only one person are called *private* goods. For example, you may purchase a magazine or newspaper, read it, and then throw it away. You may purchase food, clothing, or other goods and services for your private consumption. In each of these examples you make a decision that the benefit you receive from that good is greater than the cost of it.

Some goods are consumed by more than one person. *Public* goods provide benefit to more than one person. Books in a library, a television broadcast, a fireworks display, a college class lecture, a software program that you download onto your computer and then share with a friend, all are public goods. More than one person enjoys benefits from each of these goods without detracting from the consumption enjoyed by others. The library book is used by more than one patron in its lifetime. The television broadcast, fireworks display, and lecture are viewed by many simultaneously. A software program can be used by more than one person at the same time.

A public good is not always a good produced by the government or public sector. It is "public" because more than one person enjoys it. Public goods can be produced by the private sector, such as television broadcasts, newspapers, or computer software. Public goods can also be produced by the government or public sector, such as census data, presidential news conferences, and libraries.

Public goods are non-rival in consumption. *Non-rival* means that more than one person can share the benefit of the consumption of the good. As a result of non-rival consumption, public goods are efficiently financed through the joint cooperation of consumers. A spectacular Fourth of July fireworks display, the public library, and government agencies are financed cooperatively by individual taxpayers in the community. Individuals who benefit from the consumption of the public good must each give or pay a fair share of the total revenues needed to support it. However, financing for public goods does not necessarily have to come from taxes. Financing of public goods can also occur through user fees, donations, or advertising revenues. A movie, jointly consumed by patrons, is financed by selling movie tickets. Church worship, televangelists, and many nonprofit organizations are financed by donations. Network television broadcasts, radio stations, and many web sites are financed by advertising revenues. Newspapers are financed by selling papers and charging for advertising.

Information is a public good. Information can be shared by more than one consumer. A television broadcast, radio broadcast, and web page are viewed by more than one person simultaneously. Several copies of the same book can be sold to and read by more than one person at the same time. The same book in a library can be read by more than one patron in the same year. Information is produced for consumption by more than one person. It is typically distributed in a format for one or a few people to enjoy. Newspapers, books, CDs, and videos are produced to distribute a copy of the information to an individual or family. Each copy provides a benefit to the consumer. Each consumer, by purchasing a copy of the information, contributes to the joint financing of it. The revenue from sales pays for the costs of development, authors, programmers, editors, reporters, musicians, actors, production, and the costs of reproducing and distributing the information.

Public Good Demand

The demand or benefit from a public good is the sum of the willingness-to-pay or benefit by consumers for each unit of the good. Each consumer shares the benefit from each unit of the good. This is unlike a private good, where each consumer gets a private benefit from each unit the consumer purchases without sharing the purchase or benefit with other consumers. Therefore, with a public good the benefit is the sum of the benefits from each consumer that receives a benefit from the unit of output. This is illustrated in Table 5.1.

Table 5.1 Public Good Demand for Shared Journal Subscriptions among Three Scientists				
Number of Subscriptions	George	Greg	James	Total
1	$150	$75	$40	$265
2	$100	$40	$25	$165
3	$ 75	$30	$20	$125
4	$ 62	$25	$17	$104
5	$ 52	$20	$15	$ 87

In the fictitious example in Table 5.1, the three scientists share a laboratory and are considering jointly purchasing several journal subscriptions. The journal subscriptions would be shared among the scientists. Table 5.1 simplifies this decision by assuming that the journal subscriptions are similar and the benefit they receive from the first is the highest for all three scientists. The three scientists have a common second choice that they value less, a third choice, etc., for the five journals they are considering jointly purchasing subscriptions to.

Public goods should be jointly financed. The scientists may pool their funds to purchase more journal subscriptions than each would individually. Assume for this example that a personal subscription to each journal costs $100. If the scientists purchase journals only for their private use, then George will subscribe to two journals while Greg and James will not subscribe to any. This is because George's benefit or willingness-to-pay for two journal subscriptions is $100 each. George would pay a total of $200 for two journal subscriptions. George's consumer surplus would be $50 (the $250 in benefit minus $200 cost).

However, if the scientists pool their resources and order several subscriptions at $100 each, they will purchase four journal subscriptions. The fourth subscription has a shared benefit of $104, while the fifth subscription has a shared benefit of $87. The scientists would pay a total of $400 for the four subscriptions. Their consumer surplus would be $259 (the $659 in benefit minus $400 cost). The journals are public goods, shared by the three scientists. The scientists' public good demand and optimal number of subscriptions is shown in Figure 5.1.

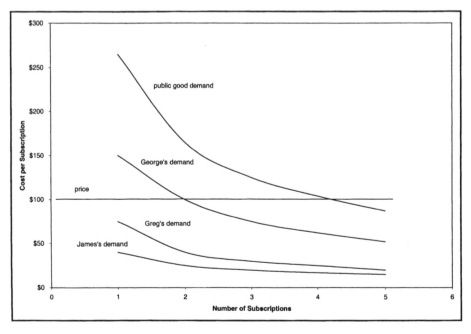

Figure 5.1. Public Good Demand for Shared Journal Subscriptions.

In Figure 5.1, the public good demand curve is the vertical summation of the three scientists' demand curves. The price line at $100 crosses George's demand curve at two subscriptions and the public good demand curve at four subscriptions.

This is an example of a special or corporate library. In this small corporate library there are three scientists who have a public good demand for journal subscriptions. In any library, there are patrons who have a public good demand for access to books, journals, databases, reference services, and other materials and services. The use of library services reflects the demand for these services by patrons. Even if patrons are not charged a price for access, they have an opportunity cost of time spent traveling to and using the services. The public good demand curve for library services can be constructed by summing the value of each patron's demand. In a corporate library there is also the benefit to the corporation of the scientists' access to the library services. New products and services developed by scientists increase the profitability of the corporation. The increase in corporate profit, over and above what the scientists view as their demand for the library, is also part of the public good demand for the corporate library services.

Estimating demand for public goods is difficult. When consumers are charged for access, we can use data on the amount they purchase to estimate their demand. For example, the number of newspapers, copies of a software program, cell phone minutes of access, or movie tickets sold can be used to estimate demand. However, when consumers are not charged for access, economists must be creative in finding metrics to use for demand analysis. The use of special, public, school, or research libraries along with the opportunity cost of this use can be helpful in determining demand for these public goods. Proxies for use include circulation, reference questions asked, interlibrary loan items requested, library web page hits, and number of library visitors.

Demand for public goods is also estimated by asking patrons or citizens to quantify the benefit they receive from the goods. For example, surveys of library patrons ask which services patrons would like increased or decreased. Surveys of citizens ask about the financing of community services. Economists have found that it can be difficult to calculate the demand for public goods from these surveys because citizens have an incentive to misrepresent the benefit they receive from services if they feel it may increase these services or increase their taxes. Finally, many public goods produced by governments are influenced by election results. Public school and public library budgets are voted on by local residents. The residents express their demand for these services by voting for or against the proposed level of spending. Although these methods of measuring the demand for public goods may be imprecise, it is important to try to assess the demand and cost of a public good to determine the efficient level of output.

Financing Public Goods

Once the efficient level of public good is determined, the remaining problem is to find a method of financing it. With private goods, the price is used to provide revenue to cover the costs of supply. With public goods, providing revenue to cover costs is more difficult. If a single price is charged, less than the optimal amount of the public good will be purchased. This was illustrated in the example of journal subscriptions for the three scientists. At a price of $100, George was willing to purchase only two journal subscriptions. James and Greg were not willing to purchase subscriptions. The problem that remains is finding a method of finance that provides $400 for the purchase of four journal subscriptions.

There are several solutions to this problem. However, one solution that will not work is to equally divide the cost by the number of patrons or the number of journal subscriptions. If each one of the three scientists were asked to pay $33.34 per journal or $133.34 per year for the four subscriptions, George and Greg would be willing to pay this but James would not. At $33.34 per subscription, James is only willing to purchase one subscription. In addition, if James were asked to pay $133.34 for the four subscriptions, he would not pay it.

Each of the scientists has a total benefit from the four journal subscriptions and a price such that each would purchase four subscriptions. James receives $102 in benefit from the four subscriptions and $17 from the fourth subscription. James is willing to pay as much as $102 for the subscriptions or to purchase four subscriptions if charged $17 per subscription. George is willing to pay as much as $387 for the subscriptions or to purchase four subscriptions if charged $62 per subscription. Greg is willing to pay as much as $170 for the subscriptions or to purchase four subscriptions if charged $25 each. Any charge less than or equal to the total each scientist is willing to pay for the four subscriptions and a price less than or equal to the price they are willing to pay together to purchase four subscriptions that provides a total of $400 to finance the subscriptions will work. For example, if George pays $200 and Greg and James pay $100 each for the bundle of four subscriptions, they will have a total of $400. Each scientist is willing to pay this much for the four journals. An alternative method of financing is to charge George a price of $60 per journal, Greg $25 per journal, and James $15. This provides a total of $100 per journal. At a price of $60 George would purchase four journals, at a price of $25 Greg would purchase four journals, and at a price of $15 James would purchase four journals. Each scientist has a price that he would be willing to pay to purchase the optimum number of journals.

Public goods can be financed by individual "prices," fees for access, tax revenue, or donations. To effectively charge consumers for access there must be a way to exclude individuals who do not pay the fee. Exclusionary public goods, sometimes referred to as *club* goods, are those public goods from which individuals can be excluded, at a reasonable cost, from consuming or benefiting. This property enables these goods to be financed in whole or in part through user fees. Movies, newspapers, public swimming pools, toll roads, Internet service providers, cable television, and video rentals are all examples of exclusionary public goods. Only those consumers who purchase a movie ticket or newspaper, pay the ISP access fee, subscribe to cable television, or rent videos are able to enjoy consuming the public good. Other potential consumers are excluded.

Sometimes, although an exclusionary fee could be charged, it is not, in order to ensure access. Video stores charge a fee to borrow videos. Public libraries could charge a fee to borrow books. Public libraries do not charge book borrowing fees, to ensure access by all patrons to the books. Instead, public libraries are financed through tax revenue. The community decides, through representatives or a vote on the library budget, how much tax revenue it will use to support the public library.

Nonexclusionary public goods are those from which individuals cannot be effectively excluded. Examples of nonexclusionary public goods include fireworks displays, some public parks, broadcast television, radio, local roads, and street corner evangelists. In each case, it is difficult or costly to exclude certain consumers from benefiting from the good. Local governments could post toll collectors at every intersection, but the cost of this policy would be much greater than the revenue received. Unlike exclusionary public goods, for which user fees pay many of the costs of production, other financing must be used to pay for the production of nonexclusionary goods. Government taxes pay for fireworks displays, public parks, and local roads. Broadcast television and radio sell advertising to pay for themselves.

Nonexclusionary public goods are frequently supplied by governments and paid for by taxes. Because of the nonexclusionary character of these goods, the only way to pay for their production is to make payment compulsory. A public road will be used by many members of the community; therefore, the community taxes all its members to pay to build and maintain the road. Many public finance economists believe that the primary responsibility of governments is to provide nonexclusionary public goods. However, although governments can collect taxes to pay for public goods, the problems of how much of the public good to provide, how much benefit citizens get from these public goods, and how much each citizen should be taxed are difficult to resolve.

Public goods can also be financed by donations. This method of finance, however, often results in a level of output less than the socially efficient level. When public goods are financed by voluntary contributions, such as public television and radio, the organization must rely on donors to make a fair assessment of the marginal benefit they receive from the public good and contribute this amount. However, donors may give less than their fair share or get what economists call a free ride by enjoying the public benefit financed by the donations of others. Donor free-riding results in less than the economically efficient level of the public good being produced. Nonprofit organizations exert social pressure on individuals to prevent free-riding. Public television and radio stations give out free coffee mugs, books, and other items to reward those who pay their fair share. Donors to universities, museums, and other organizations receive recognition for their donation in a university newsletter or on a wall plaque.

Information as a Public Good

Information is a public good that can be exclusionary or nonexclusionary. Information as a nonexclusionary public good includes general health education. Information on the importance of washing your hands, the need for vaccinations, or the importance of safe sex can be conveyed by broadcast television, leaflets, or through schools as a nonexclusionary public good. Each individual receives the same information but does not pay to get it. In fact, there is a societal benefit from decreasing the spread of germs and viruses.

Health information is also created as an exclusionary public good to provide profit and employment to an organization. Medical treatments, new drugs, and a doctor's medical training are all exclusionary public goods. The treatment or drug is developed after a significant company investment in research and development. Patent laws ensure that the company has ownership of the intellectual property or knowledge of the medical treatment or the process for making the drug. The information or knowledge about the best treatment or drug to treat a disease is information that is likely to have an inelastic demand by patients. Likewise, a doctor invests time and resources to acquire the knowledge of how to treat patients. To patients, the information about treating their disease is a public good. Many patients may have the same illness or visit the same doctor, each paying for access to the information. In this way, medical services can be modeled as an exclusionary public good.

Information can also be partly but not fully exclusionary. Computer software must be purchased to download on your personal computer. Consumers who purchase the software contribute toward financing the research and development of programmers needed to create the software. In this case, the software program is an exclusionary public good. Computer software piracy occurs when consumers share the software program by allowing friends to download it onto their computers. The company that owns the patent to the software program does not receive revenue from software piracy.

Information is distributed through disks, paper, wires, or airwaves. The information is a public good, but the distribution mechanism makes it exclusionary or nonexclusionary. If access is exclusionary, the costs of producing the information, in addition to the costs of distributing it, can be paid for. Distribution by print can involve a transaction of payment for the information. Photocopying print information breaks the "exclusionarity" of it; however, photocopying requires access to a photocopier, the opportunity cost of time, and the cost of paper and toner. Electronic media, particularly in a networked environment, make distribution without payment to the intellectual property owner more likely. Violating copyright by sharing a copy of a computer software program on disks is easier, and involves a greater amount of information shared, than sharing print information by using a photocopier. The Internet enables consumers who are willing to violate copyright easy access to text, pictures, and software.

The alternative to financing information by access fees is to charge for advertising. Nonexclusionary information products are typically financed by advertising. Television, radio, web pages, and even some long-distance telephone services receive revenue from advertising. In these cases, the information producer sells access to consumers' time by other information producers. Consumers must "spend" time seeing commercials to access the information or entertainment they want. Recently some long-distance telephone service providers have eliminated access or per-minute charges; instead the caller must listen to commercials to "buy" long-distance telephone minutes. Newspapers and magazines provide a balance of raising revenue from the price of the good and from advertising.

Consumers would be better off if the commercials did not interfere with their viewing of programs, but the commercials pay for the production. Sometimes consumers can get or purchase commercial-free access. Radio stations will advertise the number of songs played in a row without commercials to gain more listeners. In this example, the radio station may be able to increase its commercial fees if it can demonstrate that it can provide companies with access to a greater number of listeners. For an additional fee, cable television offers movie channels where popular movies are shown without commercial interruption. This illustrates that under some circumstances consumers are willing to pay for access instead of spending time viewing unwanted information.

Summary

Information is a public good. Public goods are non-rival in consumption, benefiting more than one consumer. Information in a newspaper, book, magazine, television, radio, or online can be consumed by more than one person at the same time. In fact, this consumption does not detract from the consumption of others.

It is difficult to measure the demand for public goods. Because many consumers are using the same information simultaneously, it is difficult to measure the value to any one consumer. Even with exclusionary public goods, suppliers must guess at consumers' willingness–to-pay. This makes it likely that the supply of public goods will be less than the pareto optimum level.

Having more than one consumer of the same good means that the costs of producing a public good should be shared among the consumers. Exclusionary public goods share the cost by charging an access fee. Nonexclusionary public goods receive revenue from donations, taxes, or advertising. Information goods can be financed by one or more of these revenue sources.

Chapter 6

Externalities

Externalities occur when the production or consumption of a good generates benefits or costs to individuals other than the consumers or producers of that good. *Negative externalities* are social costs from the production or consumption of a good in excess of the direct costs of production. Pollution, computer viruses, false gossip, crowded roads, talking in the library or movie theater, and excessive junk mail are all examples of negative externalities. In each case a social cost is imposed on someone who is not directly determining consumption or production in the market. *Positive externalities* are social benefits from the production or consumption of a good or service in excess of the direct benefits in the market. Your neighbor's lawn care, inoculations against infectious diseases, good news, and charitable contributions to nonprofit organizations are all positive externalities. In each example there are individuals, other than the buyers and sellers of the good, who receive a benefit from the good or service.

For both types of externalities, market prices, which connect buyers and sellers, do not include the external benefits or costs imposed on other members of society. For this reason, the decisions made by consumers and producers do not reflect the full social benefit or cost of the good or service. As a result, the socially efficient level of output may be greater or less than the competitive market equilibrium.

Many information goods and services exhibit externalities. Often individuals do not want to read, see, or hear information—junk mail, advertisements, sexually explicit material on television, bad news, talking by others in the library—but receive it regardless of their wishes. In these examples, the consumption by individuals who purchase the products of advertising or want to receive the information cannot be separated from that of those who do not want to receive it. As a result, the consumption of the information by consumers of it imposes a negative externality on those who do not want it.

At other times, information that may provide a useful benefit to others is not received by them. For example, information on the quality of products, class notes for the final exam, all helpful information, may or may not be given to all those who could receive a benefit from it. The consumers of the information, those who have researched the quality of a product or attended the class to take notes, do not always have the ability or incentive to share this information with others. The information, which has a positive externality on others, is not disseminated to all the individuals who could benefit from it.

Negative Externalities

Negative externalities are by-products of markets for goods or services. They are social costs produced as the result of market behavior but not incorporated into the decisions of producers and consumers participating in the market. When paint is produced and consumed, the negative externality of pollution is also produced. When travelers use roads for their personal benefit, they do not consider the social costs of the congestion on other travelers. When direct mail is sent to potential consumers, direct marketing firms find it difficult to avoid households uninterested in purchasing their products. When gossip is passed around among friends, the friends rarely consider the negative externality it may have on the subject of the gossip. In each case a social cost is imposed on someone who is not directly determining consumption or production in the market. As a result, the competitive equilibrium level of output of the good or service typically exceeds the socially efficient level.

An excellent example of a market with a negative externality is the market for direct marketing, or junk mail. Direct marketing mail provides some people with useful information about available goods. But it is a negative externality to others who do not want to spend the time to review and discard it. This is the result of a market in which the individuals who pay for the junk mail or receive the most direct benefit from it, direct marketing firms, are not the individuals who receive it. The companies who produce the junk mail impose costs on others who are not paying for it or directly participating in the production or distribution of it.

The benefit that direct marketing firms receive from junk mail is the increased sales resulting from the advertising. The cost of junk mail is the cost of paper and postage to produce and deliver it. As long as the expected benefit of increased profit to the owners of the direct marketing firm exceeds the cost of sending direct mail, they will produce and mail it. The level of junk mail sent will be determined by the expected marginal benefit to the direct marketing firms that pay for it, and it is only indirectly influenced by the individuals who receive the mail.

We can approximate the cost of the externality by measuring the cost of the time spent by individuals who involuntarily receive direct mail and do not purchase the products. For example, assume that every piece of junk mail takes 10 seconds to open, review, and discard. Also assume that the opportunity cost or value of time for the average person is $36 per hour. The external cost of each piece of junk mail is $0.10 per piece. In other words, the recipient "spends" $0.10 worth of time for each piece of junk mail received. If you receive five pieces of junk mail a day, you must spend $0.50 of your time to open and discard it. Of course you may open more or less junk mail, and the value of your time may be more or less than $36 per hour; however, these assumptions provide reasonable approximations for the average amount of junk mail, average time, and average value of the time.

The financial cost of junk mail to the direct marketing firm is the cost of labor and paper plus the cost of postage. Assume that this equals $0.30 per piece of junk mail. The cost to society per piece of junk mail is the marginal social cost, which equals the financial cost to the direct marketing firm plus the external cost to individuals who receive it. In our example, the marginal social cost of junk mail equals $0.40 per piece.

Junk mail also has a benefit. Direct marketing firms receive profit from the items they sell via junk mail. Without loss of generality, we can assume that the additional profit from direct marketing decreases for each additional mailing; that is, the marginal benefit curve for junk mail slopes downward. The direct marketing firm will distribute mail first to individuals they believe will be the most likely to purchase the product. Nonprofit organizations send mail asking for contributions first to individuals who have given money in the past because they are the most likely to respond to a request for contributions. As more mail is sent, there is a decreasing chance that individuals receiving the mail will purchase goods or make a contribution to the organization.

In Figure 6.1, the equilibrium level of junk mail is at 40,000 pieces. This is the intersection of the marginal cost (supply) curve and the marginal benefit (demand) curve. This equilibrium is the level of junk mail that maximizes the direct marketing firm's profit. To maximize profit a direct marketing firm will send out mail as long as the marginal benefit, or expected profit, from that mail exceeds the marginal cost of $0.30. For example, the 30,000th piece of mail gives an expected profit of $0.40 at a cost of $0.30 for a net profit of $0.10. When the marginal benefit of the next mailing is less than the marginal cost, as occurs above 40,000 pieces, the firm stops sending out additional mailings.

However, direct marketing firms do not consider the social costs, or negative externality, imposed on consumers who must spend time discarding the junk mail. The *marginal social cost* is the cost to producers of a good plus the costs of any negative externality. If the cost imposed on receivers of the junk mail is considered, the social cost is $0.40 per letter ($0.30 in mailing costs plus $0.10 of externality). Therefore, the social optimum level of junk mail is at 30,000. For all pieces mailed between 30,000 and 40,000, the marginal social cost of the piece exceeds the marginal benefit the direct marketing firm receives from it. Society (consumers and producers) would be better off if the extra 10,000 pieces of junk mail were not sent.

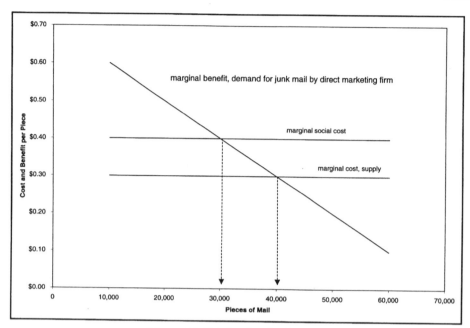

Figure 6.1. Market for Junk Mail.

Like the market for junk mail, information products that exhibit negative externalities are frequently overproduced. Producers and consumers are unlikely to consider the negative effects of their actions on others, particularly when profit or self-interest motivates actions and external costs are difficult to observe. The dissemination of information, in the form of advertising, is also difficult to selectively target or consume. The direct marketing firms cannot effectively send out their catalogues and letters only to those individuals who will purchase their products. Likewise, we cannot open only those pieces of mail advertising products we want to purchase. Information must be consumed before its value, or cost, can be determined.

Positive Externalities

Whereas negative externalities are social costs not considered by producers and consumers, positive externalities are social benefits from the production or consumption of a good or service in excess of the direct benefits received by consumers. Because these external benefits are not received by those purchasing the good or service, the external benefits are not expressed in the consumers' demand or willingness-to-pay for the good or service. As a result, consumers will purchase less of the good than is socially optimal. Inoculations for contagious diseases, education, your neighbor's lawn care, a good review of the book you recently wrote, and even junk mail for some individuals are all examples of positive externalities.

Many information goods and services have positive externalities. This is because information goods and services frequently have a benefit to individuals beyond the consumers or purchasers of these goods. Education is a good example of this. An education can benefit not only the individual receiving it but also others who benefit from having more educated members of society. Children in school are not committing crimes, educated adults make better citizens, and the more bright people there are to talk to the better educated and informed the people they talk to become.

For example, there is a positive externality of education to prevent infection by sexually transmitted diseases. The market benefit from sex education is the benefit accrued by those individuals who, as a result of the education, do not get infected. In other words, you spend the time to educate yourself on these matters to prevent becoming infected, which provides a direct benefit to you, the "consumer" of the information. The positive externality is the benefit received by individuals other than the ones receiving the direct benefit from the information. In this example, the positive externality is the benefit received by individuals who do not become infected as a result of someone receiving the education: Someone who has received the education and avoided becoming infected cannot infect someone else. Another way of understanding this is that if every infected person transmits the disease to someone else, then every person who receives the education and avoids becoming infected will be prevented from transmitting the disease to someone else. The social benefit of sex education is the sum of the benefits to those who are educated plus the positive externality to their future partners.

There is also a cost to sex education. The cost of sex education includes the cost of printing pamphlets, producing commercials, or having teachers to provide classes. The cost also includes the opportunity cost or value of the time individuals must spend to find and read the information. Sex education taught in a secondary school also includes the opportunity cost of the value of classes students did not attend or receive because of the time spent in a sex education class.

This market is shown in Figure 6.2. The socially efficient level of sex education is at 4,000 students. The equilibrium is at 3,000 students. This is because individuals who receive education only consider the benefits to themselves, not the external benefits received by future partners who will not be infected. Therefore, 1,000 fewer students will receive the education than is socially optimal.

Frequently, when there are positive externalities from the consumption of a good or service, the government provides subsidies, regulates the market, or imposes government mandates on services. In this example, government subsidies or government provision of sex education via public schools may increase the level of education to the socially efficient level. For example, in Figure 6.2 a subsidy of $5 per student will increase the level of sex education to the socially efficient level. This subsidy may take the form of mailing information to individuals at risk or providing them with education at bars, hospitals, or other locations where the opportunity cost or value of time spent acquiring the literature will be lower than having to travel to a health care provider to ask for information.

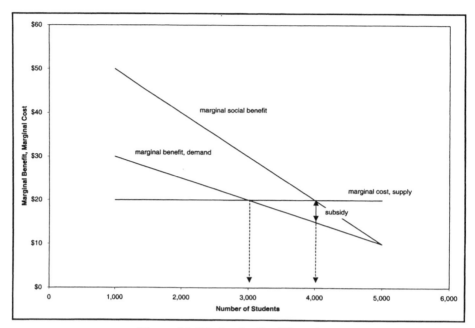

Figure 6.2. Market for Sex Education.

Many information goods are provided or subsidized by the government to correct for the underprovision of these goods that occurs when there are positive externalities. Health and safety education, consumer information, and arguably political information can all be modeled as having positive externalities; however, the government provision or subsidy of these services is not without cost. Although the existence of a positive externality implies an underprovision of these goods and services, a complete analysis of the need for government subsidies or provision requires calculating the cost of government involvement and comparing it to the benefit of correcting for the externality present.

Balancing Positive and Negative Externalities

It is also possible for the consumption or production of information goods and services to have a positive externality on some people and a negative externality on others. For example, while some people feel that sex education prevents the spread of infectious diseases and teenage pregnancy, others feel that sex education encourages premature sex among teenagers. If education makes individuals feel unjustifiably safe about their behavior, it may impose a negative externality on others by resulting in pregnancy, the spread of a sexually transmitted disease, or emotional trauma from premature sexual behavior.

Junk mail, which has a negative externality on those who dislike it, has a positive externality on the recipients who enjoy it or find it useful. Some people simply enjoy receiving mail, regardless of where it is from. Others are consumers of the products advertised via direct mail and receive consumer surplus from their purchases. Because the consumer surplus is a benefit in excess of the profits or revenues received by the direct marketing firm, it is a positive externality from the use of direct marketing mail. If we assume that there is a direct relationship between the amount of junk mail and the purchases of these consumers—for example, each 100 pieces of mail may result in one item sold—then the consumer surplus from every item sold produces a positive externality for every 100 pieces of direct mail. This consumer surplus is not included in the profits of direct marketing firms because it is the benefit consumers receive over and above the amount they pay for their purchases. As the amount of junk mail increases, the expected purchases per 100 pieces decline, as does the consumer surplus. Therefore, the marginal external benefit curve for junk mail must be downward sloping.

The marginal private benefit from junk mail is the profit received by producers from sales. The marginal private benefit is added to the marginal external benefit to get the marginal social benefit curve in Figure 6.3. Each piece of junk mail provides benefits to three groups—direct marketing firms, their consumers, and those who enjoy receiving mail—and costs to two groups—direct marketing firms and those who dislike junk mail. The socially efficient level of junk mail in Figure 6.3 is 35,000 pieces, where the marginal social benefit from junk mail equals the marginal social cost from it. The socially efficient level of junk mail is less than the equilibrium level of 40,000 pieces because the value of the negative externality (nuisance of junk mail) exceeds the value of the positive externality (consumer surplus from sales plus enjoyment of junk mail). However, if the value of the positive externality were to exceed the value of the negative externality, then less than the socially efficient level of junk mail would be sent. In this case, efficient government policy would be to subsidize the delivery of junk mail!

If direct marketing firms could perfectly identify those individuals who want to receive junk mail and those who do not, then there would be no negative or positive externalities in this market. Direct marketing firms do not want to send junk mail to individuals who are annoyed by it because it is doubtful they are consumers of the products. Therefore, if they could identify those households that do not want to receive junk mail, the direct marketing firms would save the cost of mailing to them by removing these households from their mailing lists. Likewise, if the firms could predict who would purchase the products advertised, these firms could send mail only to those households and, for the last piece of mail sent, the marginal cost of sending to that household would equal the marginal benefit or profit the firm would receive from it. At equilibrium, the consumer surplus of the last unit purchased would equal 0 and there would be no positive externality. Unfortunately, direct marketing firms cannot perfectly predict which households want to receive mailings and which do not.

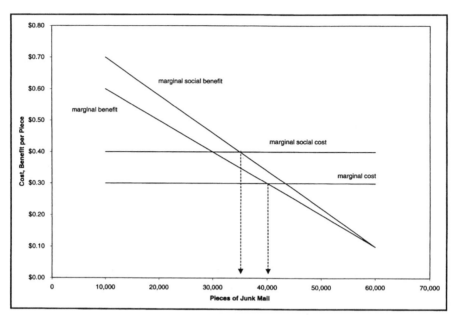

Figure 6.3. Externalities and Market for Junk Mail.

Summary

As shown in the examples in this chapter, many information products and services have positive externalities, negative externalities, or both. When externalities are present, the socially efficient level of output will be different from the market equilibrium. In the case of negative externalities, the economically efficient level of output is less than the equilibrium level. In the case of a positive externality, the economically efficient level of output is greater than the socially efficient level. When both are present, the relative strengths of positive and negative externalities determine whether the socially efficient level is more than, less than, or equal to the market equilibrium.

When externalities are present, government policy may be able to correct the market failure. With negative externalities, government regulation, taxes, or education programs that promote a reduction in the consumption of a good or service, such as unsafe sex, may decrease the level of output to the socially efficient level. With positive externalities, government subsidies, regulation, or education programs that promote the consumption of a good or service, such as health and safety, may increase the level of output to the socially efficient level.

Frequently, information goods and services either exhibit positive or negative externalities or promote the correction of a market failure. Because information can be shared at a relatively low cost, it can provide a benefit or cost to individuals other than those who originally purchased it. Valued information can be used by individuals other than the purchaser, so it has a positive externality, whereas false, slanderous, or negative information has a negative externality on those it affects. Negative and positive externalities can sometimes be corrected by educating market participants about their actions. Externalities resulting from pollution and unhealthy or unsafe behavior can be corrected by education, typically at a low cost relative to the social costs of the externality.

Chapter 7

Monopolies

Chapter 4 demonstrates that, in a competitive market, producers and consumers pursuing their own self-interest will produce a market in equilibrium that is economically efficient or at the pareto optimum. This is the result of suppliers competing with each other for market share and, as a result, selling at a price equal to the cost of the last unit sold. Competition is good. It keeps prices low and encourages firms to try to innovate or distinguish themselves from other suppliers.

Noncompetitive markets occur when either suppliers or consumers can control the market price and quantity sold. Usually this happens when one supplier controls the selling price of a good. The supplier restricts output, which drives up the equilibrium price and increases profit. In this case, the equilibrium will be less than the socially efficient level of output.

The market for journal subscriptions is the best example of what some believe is a noncompetitive market. Librarians and scholars are justifiably upset with scientific publishers who charge exorbitant prices. As journal prices increase, librarians must decide which journal titles to eliminate from the library's collection. This is particularly frustrating when librarians understand that the actual cost of printing another copy of a journal is far below the price the library is charged for a subscription. Yet federal copyright law ensures that journal publishers retain monopoly rights over the information contained in the journals.

Journal subscriptions seem to combine two parts of the economy, publishing and libraries, that follow two different philosophies when providing access to information. A profit-motivated publisher with exclusive rights to production of the good seems to have an unfair advantage over a librarian, who abides by the philosophy of free and open access to information. In the market for journal subscriptions, libraries are unable to afford additional subscriptions to journals that may provide benefit to their faculty, even though the cost of printing one more copy of the journal may be below the marginal benefit patrons would receive from that journal title. By definition, this implies a social inefficiency.

A *monopoly* is a producer that is the only supplier to a market. In this case, the monopolist has control over price and quantity sold in the market and may be able to increase profit by charging exorbitantly high prices and thereby prevent the market from achieving the socially efficient level of output. At the higher monopoly price, the marginal benefit to a consumer of an additional unit of output is greater than the marginal cost, resulting in the market failing to reach the pareto optimum.

Sometimes two or more firms collude with each other to maximize profit by behaving as if the firms were one single monopolist. A *duopoly* is a market in which there are only two producers. An *oligopoly* is a group of producers that controls a market so that it is noncompetitive. It is also possible that the suppliers behave competitively while the consumers, or demanders, control price and output in a market. Although less common, this can also lead to a socially inefficient level of output. A *monopsony* is a market with only one consumer or a group of consumers colluding to pursue the best interests of the group. A consortium of libraries may behave as a monopsony. In any of these markets, either the demander or suppliers control the market price and quantity. As a result, the controlling party can set a price or quantity of output that may not be in the best interests of society.

Monopolies are pervasive in information markets. The markets for local telephone service, mail delivery, computer operating systems, and local cable television service are all controlled by single companies. In these cases the high, fixed cost of entering the market is justification for a single firm making a profit within a market without sufficient room for a competing firm to enter. When this happens, typically the state or federal government regulates the single firm to prevent consumers from being exploited. American Telephone and Telegraph (AT&T), prior to its court-ordered breakup, was tightly regulated by the federal government. After it was proven that other companies—MCI and Sprint—could compete with AT&T in the sale of long-distance services, federal regulations relaxed but were not eliminated entirely.

In addition to these service monopolies, patent and copyright laws create monopolistic control over some information goods. These laws to protect intellectual property rights also create sole providers of information and, as a result, create monopolies over books, computer software, journals, music, pharmaceuticals, new product lines, and other goods. In each case, efficient patent and copyright law must balance the protection of intellectual property against the economic efficiencies of a competitive market. Microsoft is viewed as a monopolist in the Windows™ operating system for personal computers and may be subject to government regulation at the time this book is published.

Monopoly Demand

If there is more than one supplier, it is difficult for an individual firm to increase price without losing customers to the competition. However, when monopolists control the supply of a good, they can increase price above the competitive market price without the fear of losing customers to the competition. This price increase pushes the market to a lower level of output than is socially efficient.

The basics of monopolies can be illustrated with a simple example. In many communities, local phone installation is provided through a government-regulated single supplier or local monopoly. Consider what your local phone company might charge for phone installation if the price was not regulated. For example, assume that the marginal cost of installing a phone is the same as the average cost, for example, $75 per installation. This ignores the fixed costs of the telephone company but is not unrealistic if we consider only the costs of the installation and lump fixed costs into the cost of service. The $75 installation cost includes the cost of the wire, jacks, and other materials, and also the labor of a telephone employee coming to your home to install the phone.

If phone installation were a competitive market, then the marginal cost of $75 would represent the market supply curve. In this case, competition among firms would cause the market equilibrium price to settle at $75 per installation. Each firm would make exactly the marginal cost of an installation and would receive 0 profit. If any firm attempted to increase its price to increase profit, it would lose all of its market share to firms that continue to charge $75. This is shown in Figure 7.1

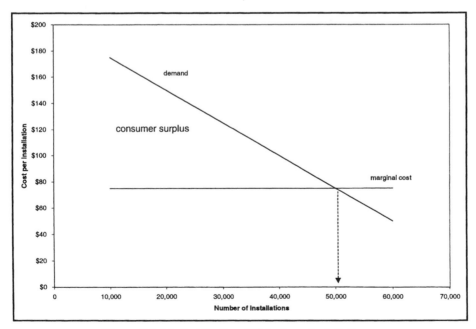

Figure 7.1. Market for Local Telephone Installations.

The area above the marginal cost and below the demand curve is the consumer surplus in a competitive market. Consumer surplus is left to consumers in a competitive market because individual firms are prevented, by market forces, from increasing price above the equilibrium. However, a profit-maximizing monopolistic firm will extract this surplus from consumers to increase profit. Maximum profit is essentially the most revenue that can be taken from what would be consumer surplus in a competitive market. Using the above example, if the local phone company were an unregulated monopoly it would raise the price of an installation to increase profit.

Table 7.1 shows that the company maximizes profit by setting its price equal to $138 per installation and selling 25,000 installations. The *marginal revenue* from an installation is the change in revenue, $\delta(PQ)$, divided by the change in installations sold, δQ, as a result of the price being lowered. The marginal revenue is the additional revenue that the producer expects to receive when the price is lowered and one more unit of output is sold. The profit-maximizing quantity is also the quantity such that the marginal revenue from an installation is about equal to the marginal cost. If we were to calculate the marginal revenue from an increase in demand of 24,999 to 25,000, we would observe that the marginal revenue is $75 for the 24,999th installation, exactly equal to the marginal cost. A monopolist will increase price until the additional revenue from selling one more installation, the marginal revenue, equals the additional cost of the installation, the marginal cost.

The monopolist's pricing policy results in a level of output less than the socially efficient level of output. This is illustrated in Figure 7.2. For each installation between 25,000 and 50,000, the marginal benefit to a consumer exceeds the marginal cost of the installation. For example, the 30,000th installation has a marginal benefit of $125 to a consumer and a marginal cost of only $75. This means there is $50 of net benefits that society could receive if this consumer was allowed to purchase an installation at cost. However, if the monopolist is restricted to charging only one price in this market or cannot discern between consumers and therefore must charge all consumers the same price, the monopolist will lose profit by reducing the price. As a result, all net benefits between the 25,000th installation and the 50,000th installation are lost to society. This social loss, called *deadweight loss*, equals the shaded area in Figure 7.2. The deadweight loss is the sum of the consumer surplus that society could have received if the price where set equal to $75.

	**Table 7.1**
	**The Market for Telephone Installations**
Demand	Marginal Cost	Price	Revenue	Total Cost	Profit		Marginal Revenue
10,000	$75	$175	$1,750,000	$750,000	$1,000,000		
20,000	$75	$150	$3,000,000	$1,500,000	$1,500,000		$125
24,000	$75	$140	$3,360,000	$1,800,000	$1,560,000		$90
25,000	$75	$138	$3,437,500	$1,875,000	$1,562,500		$78
26,000	$75	$135	$3,510,000	$1,950,000	$1,560,000		$73
30,000	$75	$125	$3,750,000	$2,250,000	$1,500,000		$60
40,000	$75	$100	$4,000,000	$3,000,000	$1,000,000		$25
50,000	$75	$75	$3,750,000	$3,750,000	$0		
60,000	$75	$50	$3,000,000	$4,500,000			

Diagrams similar to Figures 7.1 and 7.2 can be drawn for all noncompetitive markets. In each case, as firms are able to push prices above and output below the competitive market equilibrium, profits are gained at the loss of economic efficiency. Consumers with a lower marginal willingness-to-pay will be excluded from the market to increase monopoly profits.

NORTHEAST COMMUNITY COLLEGE LIBRARY

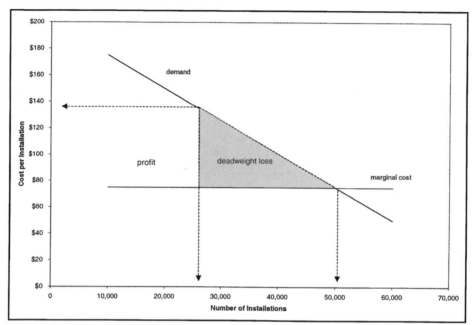

Figure 7.2. Monopoly Pricing of Local Telephone Installations.

Natural Monopolies

Although monopolies are profitable, it is difficult for a monopoly to exist. Whenever one firm is making significant profits, entrepreneurs are likely to enter the market and compete with the existing profitable firm. Monopolies are more likely to exist when either the government ensures their existence through regulation or the structure of costs is such that one large supplier is likely to dominate the market and thereby become a monopolist. Many information goods and services have one or both factors working to create a monopolistic market.

In an industry with high fixed costs, declining average costs may result in *a natural monopoly*. A natural monopoly occurs when a firm must make a large fixed investment to enter the industry and marginal costs are low compared with this fixed investment. As output increases, average cost per unit decreases. As a result, a large single supplier can sell output at a lower price and drive out potential competitors. Public utilities, local telephone service, and cable companies are common examples of potential natural monopolies. In each case there is a large fixed investment of a network of telephone, cable, electric, or gas lines along with a fixed investment of the power plant, cable television company, or telephone switchboard. Compared with these fixed investments, the cost of connecting one additional user is low.

Figure 7.3 shows the cost curves for cable service. It assumes that the fixed investment for a cable network is $10 million and the marginal cost of a connection is $30 per household.

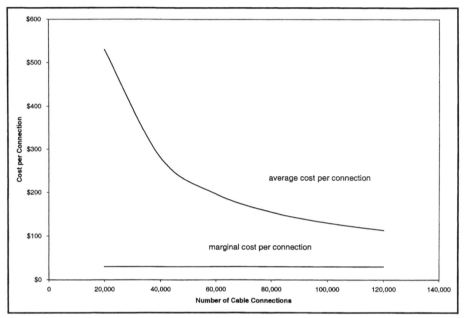

Figure 7.3. Cable Company as Natural Monopoly.

Given the large fixed costs of the cable network and the relatively lower marginal cost of a connection, the average costs for a cable company are declining. The larger a single cable company becomes, the lower the average cost of connecting an additional home is. As a result, one large firm can drive prices lower than any other small firm can match. Under our assumptions, the fixed investment of $10 million is simply too large for the market to support two competing firms.

In this case, the market equilibrium is for one large cable company to dominate service in the market. As a result, the one dominant firm in a market can set prices at a level just low enough to discourage smaller firms from competing with it and yet high enough to make a profit. In the absence of government regulation, the price will be greater than the average cost or break-even price and less than or equal to the single-price monopolist's price where marginal revenue equals marginal cost. Since the resulting price will be above the marginal cost, $30, there will be deadweight loss in this market. Even though the cost of connecting an additional consumer to the network would be only $30, the cable company is unwilling to lower its price for all consumers to this level.

Books, journals, software, and other electronic and print products frequently have downward-sloping average cost curves. The large fixed investments for an individual book title or journal issue are the "first-copy" costs. For a book, first-copy costs include the author's time and the publisher's set-up costs of editing and printing the first copy. The marginal cost is the additional cost for printing, binding, and shipping one more copy of the book. For electronic products, the first-copy costs include the time of the programmer and other fixed costs for the first copy of a program. The marginal cost is the additional cost of copying, packaging, and shipping one more copy of the program.

Although print and electronic products have downward-sloping average cost curves, they are not natural monopolies. This is because although the initial production of a book or software program requires a large fixed investment, it is possible, for those willing to violate copyright law, to make copies at a low marginal cost. For any given book or software program, competitors need only a photocopy machine or personal computer to make copies for possible sale. Potential competitors do not have the same high fixed or first-copy costs of the original publisher. However, in the absence of laws protecting intellectual property, no publishers, authors, or inventors would be willing to create intellectual property if they felt they could not receive a fair market return for their time and effort.

Patent and copyright laws protect the intellectual property of authors and inventors. However, in protecting these rights, the laws create monopolies over specific products. Patent and copyright laws enable the owners of intellectual property to be the sole suppliers of that property. I am the owner of the expression of the ideas contained in this book. As the owner, I pass on my ownership to the publisher, who in turn becomes the monopolistic supplier of this book. Copyright law ensures that our monopoly is maintained for my lifetime plus 70 years. Patent law enforces similar monopoly rights over a shorter period, typically 15 years, for inventions.

The problem of compensating individuals for their intellectual property, and monopoly pricing, is illustrated in Figures 7.4 and 7.5. Figure 7.4 shows the market for intellectual output, for example, books, computer software, pharmaceutical drugs, or any other output protected by copyright or patent law. The demand curve **D** in Figure 7.4 is the lifetime marginal benefit to consumers of this good. The creator's ability to exploit this market, or price charged, depends on the length of the patent or copyright, the breadth of copyright—that is, how similar a substitute product by other firms is allowed—and the value of the good or service to consumers. Assume that the initial price that maximizes profit for the copyright owner is **P.** The level of output sold at price **P** is **Q.** This price results in a deadweight loss equal to area **ABC.**

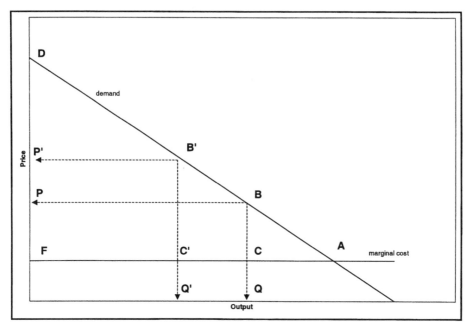

Figure 7.4. Market for Output of Intellectual Property.

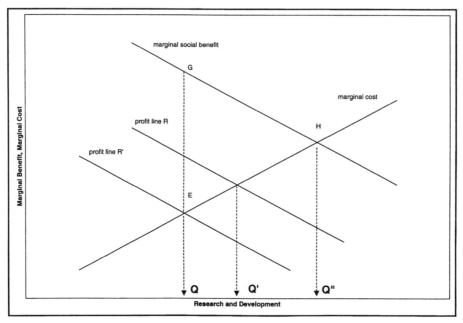

Figure 7.5. Market for Research and Development.

Figure 7.5 shows the market for research and development or creativity. The supply or marginal cost of research and development is the cost of the authors' or inventors' time and effort in writing books, creating computer programs, or developing new pharmaceutical drugs. The marginal social benefit curve in Figure 7.5 represents the maximum net benefit possible from a given creative activity. This is the maximum consumer surplus possible if the output of this creative activity were sold at its marginal cost. For example, the net benefit possible in Figure 7.4 is area **ADF**, the maximum consumer surplus. Each creative endeavor has a cost equal to the time and effort of the inventor or author and a potential benefit equal to the consumer surplus of the consumers of the output: the books, software, and drugs created.

The profit line **R** in Figure 7.5 is the expected profit line possible for the company engaged in research and development. Expected profits are less than the marginal benefit because, in this example, not all consumer surplus can be transferred into profit. Given the expected profit from creative activity, **R,** and the marginal cost of time and effort by authors and inventors, there is an equilibrium in Figure 7.5 where **Q** is time spent employed in creating intellectual property. However, since inventors do not consider the consumer surplus from their endeavors, **Q** is less than the socially efficient amount of research and development, **Q'**. All hours employed in creating new books, drugs, and computer programs between **Q** and **Q"** would result in a potential consumer surplus greater than the cost to the company, author, or inventor. The resulting deadweight loss is represented by area **EGH.**

To improve social efficiency in Figure 7.5, additional profit must be made by creators of intellectual property. Additional profit may be possible through strengthening the copyright and patent laws to further protect intellectual property rights. As a result, higher profits are possible, represented by a shift from profit line **R** to **R'**, and an increase in the amount spent on research and development from **Q** to **Q'**.

However, stronger intellectual property laws increase the monopolistic exploitation possible by authors and inventors shown in Figure 7.4. Stronger laws may take the form of lengthening the period of time over which copyrights and patents can be enforced; legislating against substitute goods; or a tighter enforcement of existing laws to prevent illegal copying of computer software, books, and journals. As a result, stronger laws enable creators to increase the price on output from **P** to **P'**, lowering the number of units of output sold to **Q'**, and increasing the deadweight loss from **ABC** to **AB'C'**. Although the number of hours and effort in creative endeavor increase, lowering deadweight loss, the amount of output of any individual creation may decrease and thereby increase deadweight loss.

Optimal intellectual property right laws must balance the compensation of authors, inventors, and companies investing in research and development with the benefits to consumers. Although strengthening laws increases creative effort, it also increases the capacity for monopolistic exploitation. Conversely, although weaker copyright and patent laws offer consumer access to lower prices and substitute products, they decrease the time and effort spent by authors, inventors, and companies and may decrease the quality of creative output. A partial solution to this problem is to allow producers to charge different prices to different consumers or groups of consumers for the same good. Multi-price suppliers are able to extract a greater amount of consumer surplus as profit and therefore are given a greater financial incentive to engage in creative efforts.

Multi-Price Suppliers

Products are frequently sold at different prices to different consumers. Senior citizens receive discounts to purchase goods and services. Students, faculty, and libraries pay different prices for the same journal subscription. Businesses and educators pay different prices for the same computer software. Some readers pay for the first edition in hardcover, while others wait for the lower-priced paperback or used copies to appear at their local bookstore. Consumers in different countries pay different prices for the same pharmaceuticals.

This price differentiation allows suppliers to make greater profits by differentiating among consumers. If a supplier can segment consumer demand, it can maximize profit over each demand segment. The result is a level of profit greater than can be achieved with a single price. The result is also a greater level of output. Each market segment will purchase at a different price, with a lower price for segments with lower demand. As a result, consumers will purchase units of the output which, under a single price monopolist, consumers could not afford.

We can use the example of journal publishing to illustrate this. Table 7.2 and Figure 7.6 show the cost curves and demand for the fictitious *Journal of Economics*.

Table 7.2 Demand for *Journal of Economics*				
Price	Library Subscriptions	Faculty Subscriptions	Student Subscriptions	Total Market Subscriptions
$500	100	0	0	100
$100	140	100	0	240
$75	150	300	50	500
$50	160	600	600	1,360
$20	170	700	1,200	2,070

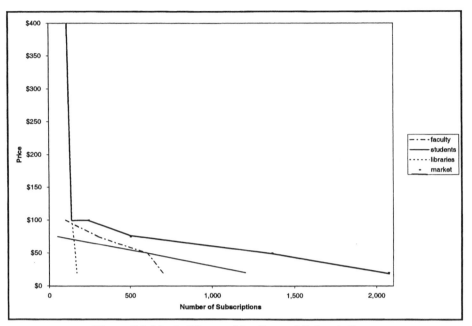

Figure 7.6. Market Demand for Journal Subscriptions.

The demand curve is divided into three segments: library, faculty, and student demand for the *Journal of Economics*. Libraries are located along the entire length of the demand curve; however, most of the higher demand along the first segment of the demand curve constitutes demand by libraries. Large research libraries have more resources and are willing to pay more for a journal subscription than any individual subscriber. In addition, a library's subscription can be viewed as a public good for many patrons whereby the sum of their marginal willingness–to-pay for the subscription is larger than the willingness-to-pay by any individual subscriber. Faculty may also be located along the entire length of the demand curve; however, faculty demand will be concentrated within the middle segment. Faculty have greater income than students but more limited resources than university libraries. The final segment of the demand curve will include most of the students in economics. These students have a lower willingness–to-pay for an economics journal because they have more limited resources than faculty and libraries. Of course there are several other factors that influence library, faculty, and student willingness-to-pay for the *Journal of Economics*, including tastes, availability of the journal in the university library, and the number of faculty and students in the economics department.

The publisher of this or any other journal can maximize profits by selling subscriptions to the different groups of consumers at different prices. The publisher maximizes profit by segmenting the market into the libraries, faculty, and student groups and charging a different profit-maximizing price to each market segment.

Profit is maximized by setting marginal revenue equal to marginal cost in each market segment. In this example, the publisher charges libraries a price of $500 for a subscription, faculty a price of $50, and students a price of $20. Libraries purchase 100 subscriptions, faculty purchase an additional 300 subscriptions, and students purchase an additional 600 subscriptions. Profit is the difference between revenues net of marginal cost for each of the three market segments and the fixed costs of production.

Multi-price publishers or monopolists can carve out a larger piece of consumer surplus than if they charged a single, common price to all consumers. Profit is maximized over each market segment, producing a higher total profit than maximizing profit using one price over the entire demand curve. With a single-price monopolist, all consumers would have to pay the same high price and, as a result, consumers with a lower willingness-to-pay—faculty and students—would be prevented from participating in the market. However, with the ability to segment the market, the price can be lowered for groups with lower demand, thereby enabling the publisher to extract additional profit from the low-demand segments.

For price discrimination to work effectively, consumers must be clearly identified in different market segments. In addition, consumers who purchase the good at a lower price must be prevented from making a profit by reselling the good at a price lower than the monopolist charges in the high-demand market segments. Otherwise, monopolists will be forced to charge one price to all consumers. In the market for journals, publishers can charge faculty and students a lower price without much concern that these groups will resell journals to the library.

It should be noted that although a multi-price supplier extracts more consumer surplus into profit, the market equilibrium is closer to the socially efficient level of output then a single-price monopolist's level of output. If the marginal cost of a journal subscription is $20, then the socially efficient number of subscriptions is 2,070. However, the single-price monopolist would sell only 100 subscriptions to libraries at a price of $500 to maximize profit. The multi-price monopolist sells 1,000 subscriptions. Although this is less than half of the socially efficient level, it is significantly larger than the single-price monopolist. If the monopolist could specify a price for each individual consumer, the seller would charge each consumer its marginal willingness-to-pay and extract all the potential consumer surplus as profit. Some libraries would pay $500 for a subscription, whereas others would pay only $20, depending on their demand or willingness to pay. In the end, the market equilibrium level of output would be 2,070 copies. However, society would receive all the net social benefit in the form of profits for the publisher rather than consumer surplus.

Summary

The high fixed costs and low marginal costs of reproduction cause many information goods and services to have declining average-cost curves. Although this might result in a natural monopoly, the low marginal cost of reproduction prevents the owners of intellectual property from exploiting these markets because competitors can simply purchase one unit of the good and sell copies at a price lower than the authors' or inventors' average cost. Copyright and patent laws protect the intellectual property rights of authors and inventors, enabling them to receive compensation for their time and effort and encouraging future creative endeavors. Unfortunately, copyright and patent laws also enable suppliers of intellectual property to behave like monopolists and charge higher than marginal cost, socially inefficient prices.

The social inefficiencies caused by monopolists depend on their ability to price-discriminate, on the regulatory environment, and on the closeness of substitutes for their products. Perfect price-discriminating monopolists can achieve the socially efficient level of output; however, all societal benefits from this output become monopoly profits rather than consumer surplus.

Natural monopolies can also occur as a result of standards in a market. A standard is a way of doing something that results in all consumers or producers using the same method. As a result, the owner of the standard is established as a natural monopoly. For example, the QWERTY keyboard created for typewriters and used on personal computers is a standard in the market. Networked markets are similar to natural monopolies but have several important differences. These are examined in more detail in Chapter 14.

Chapter 8

Uncertainty and Risk

Uncertainty creates a market for information. When individuals or firms are uncertain about future events, the quality of products, or the honesty of others, they look to purchase information to reduce uncertainty. Information decreases risk. Risk is the potential for loss when uncertain future events may cause economic harm. Wetter or drier weather influences the supply of agricultural products, medical treatments sometimes work and sometimes do not, a company's value is influenced by the actions of managers and employees, as is the quality of the goods they make. Most markets involve some risk. The markets for agricultural goods, health care, company stocks, and consumer electronics are all influenced by the uncertainty of future events, quality of products, and honesty of individuals.

In some markets, information may be available but producers may not be willing to release it to consumers. A producer may get a better price if he can hide product defects from consumers. Uninformed or misinformed consumers tend to make poor decisions about a product's value. As a result, they are reluctant to buy goods and services, reducing the number of transactions in a market.

Information markets are, by definition, susceptible to problems of imperfect information. Information consumers cannot test the quality of books, magazines, movies, videotapes, or legal or consulting services they want until after they have bought them. They buy a book without fully knowing the quality of the authorship or the services of a lawyer without knowing in advance how valuable that lawyer's services will be. For each of these goods and services, however, there are market mechanisms to correct for imperfect information. Book and movie reviews help us determine the value to us of a book, movie, or videotape. Reading a particular magazine gives us a basis on which to predict the quality of future issues. Likewise, remedial legal action is available if the consulting services we paid for are substandard. Professional association membership, the testimony of previous clients, and the provider's education and experience are all clues to the level of quality information consumers can expect.

Information markets also evolve to correct for problems of imperfect information. Consumer magazines, movie reviews, legal guides, reputation, and word-of-mouth advertising all result from consumers' need to know about the quality of a good or service. Likewise, credit reporting agencies, medical history and insurance doctor exams, and employee-provided references are information markets designed to help suppliers of credit, insurance, or jobs become better informed about their potential clients, customers, or employees.

Expectations and the Value of Information

Even when individuals face uncertainty, they have some knowledge of what future events might happen. If you purchase a used car, it may be the quality you expected or it may disappoint you and be a lemon. A farmer may expect rain tomorrow, but there is also a chance it will not rain. If you purchase stock in Microsoft, the value of the stock may increase, decrease, or remain unchanged.

For each of these possible outcomes, individuals have an expectation of the chance that any one event may happen. If you purchase stock, you may believe that its price will increase. You may also believe there is a chance that the price will decrease and a chance that the price will not change. As an investor, you have some expectation about the likelihood of each of these events occurring. Weather forecasters report the probability of rain. Consumer reports give information on how often cars require repairs. In every case there are events that occur and the probability or expectation that an event may occur.

Figure 8.1 shows a probability tree for some event occurring. Each branch of the tree represents the chance of one outcome: **A, B,** or **C.** If we are considering tomorrow's weather, **A** could be the event that the sun is shining, **B** that it will be cloudy, and **C** that it will rain. If we are considering the price of a stock that was purchased for $10 per share, **A** could represent the price rising to $11 a share, **B** could represent the price remaining constant at $10, and **C** could represent a decrease in the price to $9 per share. In this example, we are assuming that each possible outcome has the same one-third likelihood or chance of occurring.

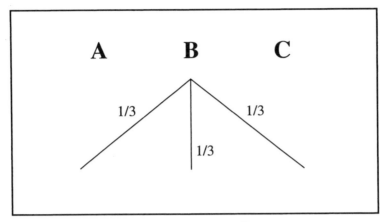

Figure 8.1. Probability Tree.

The expected value of an event is the value that an individual expects to receive based on the probability or chance that any of the outcomes might occur. For the investor, if there is a one-third chance of any of the three possible prices resulting, then the expected value of the stock is as shown in equation 8.1.

$$E = 1/3\,(\$9) + 1/3\,(\$10) + 1/3\,(\$11) = \$10 \tag{8.1}$$

In this example, the expected value of the stock is equal to its purchase price. If the investor believes that there is a better chance the price will increase, then the expected value of the stock will be higher, resulting in a possible profit for the investor if his expectations are realized.

The expected value to the farmer will be based on the chance of the three weather conditions times the value to the farmer if each of the three were realized. The crops may need rain. In this case, outcome **C** would have a higher value—equal to the increased value of the crops if there is rain—than **A** or **B**.

Information may change the expected value of an event occurring and therefore the expected value. Assume that the investor receives information that a corporation is doing better than expected. The investor may then believe that there is a 50 percent chance that the price will rise to $11 per share, a 30 percent chance that the price will remain at $10, and a 20 percent chance that the price will fall to $9 per share. The expected value is as shown in equation 8.2.

$$E = 0.50\,(\$11) + 0.30\,(\$10) + 0.20\,(\$9) = \$10.30 \tag{8.2}$$

The expected value of the stock has risen by $0.30 per share. Depending on how many shares of the stock the investor purchases, the expected value of the information is $0.30 per share multiplied by the number of shares. Note that there is still a chance that the stock price will fall or remain unchanged; however, the expected value has increased. Investors spend time and money on stock information hoping to improve their ability to determine the resulting price of a stock.

Asymmetrical Information and Markets

Markets with asymmetrical information result in economic inefficiencies. In markets with asymmetrical information, one side of the market has more information than the other side and can use the information to its advantage in extracting a higher or lower than fair price. The side of the market with less information will be less willing to engage in a transaction. For example, if buyers are uncertain about the quality of a product, even if sellers insist the product is of high quality, buyers will be reluctant to purchase it. Buyers will not be able to tell if a seller will offer a cheaper, low-quality product or a more expensive, high-quality product. As a result, efficient markets cannot occur.

A classic example of asymmetrical information is the market for used cars, first examined by George Akerlof.[1] The seller of a used car typically has more information than the buyer about the quality of the car. Sellers know how well the car starts in the winter, the last time the brakes were replaced, the age of the muffler, the location of rust spots covered by paint, and a mechanic's opinion of the engine. Buyers can only guess at the car's quality. They can kick the tires, examine its miles and age, take a test drive, and check the engine; but much of their information comes from the seller.

When asked, the seller has an incentive to misrepresent the car's quality to the buyer. If the seller can convince the buyer that the used car is of higher quality than it appears, the seller can get a better price for his car. Just as the seller has an incentive to misrepresent the quality of a used car, the buyer has little incentive to believe anything the seller says. As a result, the buyer discounts what he is willing to pay for a car by the probability the seller is misrepresenting the quality of the car to him. For a car worth $6,000 to the buyer, the buyer may only be willing to pay $5,000 simply because he cannot trust the seller to be honest.

Because all reasonably intelligent buyers assume sellers are misrepresenting the quality of their cars, sellers with "high-quality" used cars cannot sell them for what they are worth. The higher the quality of a used car, the more difficult it becomes to get paid what it is worth because all potential buyers will be suspicious of its value. As a result, few high-quality used cars are sold even though there may be buyers willing to buy them and sellers willing to sell them. The presence of imperfect information in the market prevents transactions between high-quality sellers and high-quality buyers.

Figure 8.2 illustrates the market for used cars and the result of imperfect information. In Figure 8.2, **D** is the willingness-to-pay or benefit from used cars by consumers. To illustrate the heterogeneity of used car buyers, the willingness-to-pay for each buyer is ranked from lowest to highest, or from buyers interested in purchasing low-quality used cars to buyers interested in purchasing high-quality used cars (previous demand curves ranked them from highest to lowest). The willingness-to-pay of the first buyer, or buyer of the lowest-quality used car, is $1,000. The willingness-to-pay of the last buyer is $4,500 for a used car. Sellers of used cars are ranked from those with the lowest-quality used cars to those with the highest-quality used cars along the supply curve **S.** If buyers can ascertain the quality of a used car, buyers—**D**—and sellers—**S**—will match up with each other. Buyers looking for low-quality used cars will find sellers of low-quality used cars, while buyers of higher-quality used cars will match up with sellers of higher-quality used cars. The price paid for each used car will be somewhere between the marginal benefit a buyer expects to receive from the car and the seller's supply price. For example, the lowest-quality used car in Figure 8.2 is worth $1,000 to a buyer while the seller is willing to supply it for $500. The actual price paid will be greater than $500 and less than $1,000 and will depend on the negotiating skills of the buyer and seller.

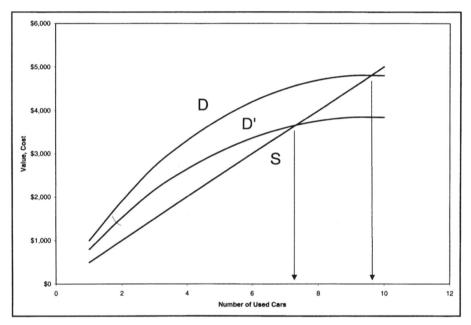

Figure 8.2. Market for Used Cars.

In the market, nine used cars will be sold. Buyers interested in used cars of higher quality cannot find sellers who are willing to part with their high-quality used car at a lower price. The tenth car has a buyer who is willing to pay $4,800 for a used car but can only find sellers of used cars willing to sell at $5,000.

Because used-car buyers do not know with certainty the quality of a car, they expect a level of benefit less than **D.** For example, if buyers receive a benefit or value of $4,000 from a "good" used car, but believe that there is a 20 percent chance that the car is a dud or that there is something wrong with the car, then the value expected will be less than $4,000. If buyers believe that there is an 80 percent chance that the car is worth $4,000 and a 20 percent chance that the car is worth $0, then the expected benefit or value of the used car would be $3,200

(0.80 X $4,000 + 0.20 X $0). Buyers will discount their willingness-to-pay by the chance that the used car is a dud. The curve **D'** in Figure 8.2 represents buyers' expected value from used cars.

Without perfect information, seven is the number of used cars sold. However, nine is the socially efficient level of used car sales. Owners of used cars between seven and nine have a relatively high supply price. This is because they perceive their cars as high-quality used cars and are only willing to sell them at a relatively high price. While some used car buyers have a benefit, **D,** which is greater than the price at which sellers between seven and nine are willing to sell their cars at, the asymmetry of information in this market prevents these transactions from occurring. Buyers are unwilling to trust sellers enough to believe that their cars are as high a quality as sellers advertise them to be. In markets with imperfect information, high-quality goods become more difficult to sell because buyers are reluctant to trust sellers.

Although markets with imperfect information can result in inefficiencies, there are also market corrections to these inefficiencies. If buyers can acquire sufficient information about the value of goods, then market inefficiencies can be mitigated to some degree. Reading a popular consumer magazine on the value of a particular used car and taking the car to a mechanic are ways in which buyers can acquire more information. Inefficiencies can also be resolved if sellers offer proof of product quality. Sellers of high-quality used cars may provide prospective buyers with detailed service and maintenance records or with the name of their mechanics to convince buyers of the value of the car. Sellers may also offer money-back warranties if problems arise within a limited time period. The warranty may never be enforced but serves as a mechanism to signal the quality of the good.

The problem of imperfect information is prevalent in many, if not all, markets to varying degrees. Markets that suffer from imperfect information include new as well as used cars, electronic goods, computer software, stocks and bonds, health care, and over-the-counter and prescription drugs. In each case, the supplier or producer of the good has an incentive to misrepresent it as being of higher quality than it may actually be because consumers cannot accurately judge the value of the good until after it has been purchased and used. As a result, consumers of these goods have a natural distrust of sellers. Market solutions to imperfect information include warranties, guarantees, good reputations, and name brands. Warranties and guarantees offer an additional contract to the buyer, which ensures the quality of the good. Good product reputations and established name brands help ensure quality based on a historical record of quality. Low-quality producers who repeatedly misrepresent the quality of their goods to consumers are unable to attract repeat buyers, develop bad reputations, and ultimately go out of business. Good reputations—gained from years of selling high-quality, reliable products—give a signal to potential customers.

Nonprofit organizations can also signal higher-quality service for goods that are difficult for consumers to judge. Child care, nursing home care, and helping the underprivileged or indigent are examples of goods the quality of which is difficult to determine. Parents may investigate the quality of a child care agency but cannot remain with their child to observe the quality of care their child gets. Likewise, when you make a contribution to the Salvation Army or American Red Cross, it is difficult to observe the quality of services provided to the poor or others who benefit from the services your donation pays for. If these services were provided by commercial organizations with the explicit goal of making a profit, it is likely that the quality of service might be reduced to increase profits. However, given that these services are provided by nonprofit organizations, with a goal of providing high-quality service and not a goal of increasing profits, consumers and donors to these organizations feel they can trust the stated quality of services provided.

Solutions to markets with asymmetrical information frequently come from within the market. Sometimes, however, government intervention is necessary to ensure that uninformed consumers are protected. Such government regulations include product safety laws, false advertising laws, and "lemon" laws to prevent fraud. In New York State, "lemon laws" prevent car dealers from selling poor-quality cars that break down within the first 90 days after purchase. Government regulations also include certification for doctors, lawyers, plumbers, teachers, and other professionals. The Food and Drug Administration regulates prescription and nonprescription drugs in an attempt to prevent consumers of medicines from purchasing low-quality or dangerous drugs that do not provide the benefits their manufacturers advertise.

Although these government regulations protect consumers from dishonest sellers, regulations are not without cost. FDA approval prevents potentially lifesaving drugs from being used for several years until approval is received. Lemon laws prevent individuals who are willing to take a risk on a potentially low-quality car from doing so. Certification of professionals raises barriers to entry by potential competitors and, therefore, may limit the supply of services and result in higher prices. An economic analysis of each of these government regulations and its impact on the market must weigh the benefits provided to consumers of these products, which presumably cannot be provided using existing market mechanisms, against the costs to government and industry of imposing the regulations.

Information Markets

Whenever information is bought and sold, there is the potential for the problem of imperfect information, or asymmetrical information, to cause market failure. Information markets rely on consumers or producers telling the truth about value, quality, or cost. There is an incentive to overstate value, quality, or cost to receive a higher price. This causes the need for information markets to validate the information from the first market.

Insurance

Insurance markets are, fundamentally, markets of imperfect information. Insurance companies try to determine the potential risk of clients by getting full information from them. When clients apply for life or health insurance, they are asked to have a physical. Insurance companies search driving records and credit records and require the potential insured to fill out forms that ask for detailed information about life style, gender, employment, and financial assets. All information is used to determine the potential risk of the insured and to set a fair market premium according to that risk; the higher the risk, the higher the premium.

Potential clients have a clear incentive to understate their level of risk, which is known as *adverse selection*. Adverse selection is the problem of high-risk clients misrepresenting their level of risk, paying the premiums for low-risk individuals, and thereby preventing market efficiency. High-risk clients may be smokers or have poor driving abilities, poor health, or other attributes that make them a poor insurance risk. If these individuals cannot be distinguished from those with lower risk, their presence in the "pool" of clients increases the number of accidents, deaths, and health problems to a level greater than the level of risk by the lower-risk clients. The increase in the level of accidents, deaths, and health risk requires insurance companies to pay out more in claims and, as a result, increases insurance premiums. However, if low-risk individuals have an accurate assessment of their risk, they are unwilling to pay premiums associated with individuals in a higher-risk pool. Low-risk individuals will cancel their insurance policies. Their departure from the pool of clients increases the average level of risk of the pool and necessitates a further increase in premiums. Ultimately, the problem of adverse selection will result in only high-risk individuals paying high premiums for insurance, while those with low risk are unable to find affordable insurance.

Although there are insurance companies willing to supply insurance to low-risk individuals at a reasonable price, if these clients cannot be distinguished from those with higher risk, the insurance market for low-risk individuals cannot exist. Like the market for used cars, the market for insurance will not be socially efficient. To correct for the problem of adverse selection, insurance companies check the backgrounds of potential clients to assign them to the correct risk pool. Individuals with good driving records, good health records, or who take classes in defensive driving are identified as being of a lower risk and receive discounted premiums.

A second problem common in insurance markets is *moral hazard*. The problem of moral hazard is that once clients have purchased coverage, the payout as the result of an accident may encourage them to behave carelessly or, worse, to cause an accident if they believe their payout will be greater than their loss. Insurance companies put requirements on insurance policies to prevent careless behavior. To prevent moral hazard, insurance companies require fire detectors in the home, give discounts for the successful completion of defensive driving classes, and make lower payouts to victims of car accidents who were not wearing their seatbelts at the time of the accident. Legislation—such as seat-belt laws, building codes and inspections, and drunk driving laws—also discourages careless behavior.

Education

Jacob Mincer, Michael Spence,[2] and other economists have modeled education as an investment in human capital. Students invest in their human capital by spending time acquiring an education and paying tuition in hopes of receiving a return on their investment of a higher salary or preferred occupation. Education is an investment in building a stock of knowledge to be used in later employment. As an investment, education is a durable good that depreciates. A doctor, lawyer, or librarian acquires a stock of knowledge, which will be used for many years of employment. However, as new medical skills, new laws, and new information technologies become available, the old stock of knowledge depreciates or loses value, requiring individuals to reinvest in new education or new knowledge to maintain their salaries and keep their jobs.

An investment in education also signals an individual's potential performance as an employee. Because employers want to identify capable employees prior to employment, there is a market for employee information. An education or degree is a signal to employers of the ability of a potential employee. A high school graduate may have more ability than someone who did not graduate from high school. Likewise, a college graduate may have more ability than someone who did not graduate from college. Someone with a doctorate in economics has the potential to be a better economist than someone with a master's degree. The alma mater's reputation also provides information about the training and ability of the individual. Someone with a medical degree from the University of Chicago may be a better physician than someone with a medical degree from an institution that does not have the same high standards and level of quality.

Other Information Markets

There are several other situations in which imperfect information prevents the market from achieving economic efficiency. These include the markets for religion, marriage, and employment. In the religious market there are several "sellers": priests, rabbis, sheiks, and ministers. Each "seller" believes it has perfect information about the "true" religion or method of salvation. Unlike the used car example, suppliers of religious services may be as uninformed as consumers about their religious beliefs. Consumers, with less than perfect information, must decide which is the correct religion. Obviously social efficiency cannot be attained unless everyone chooses the correct religion. However, given the inevitable lack of perfect information, it is not possible for social efficiency to improve.

The same problems of imperfect information occur in the marriage market. Dating and courtship are mechanisms used to acquire more information about a potential spouse. When satisfactory information about a potential spouse is acquired, the couple marries, in part to prevent the mate from continuing to seek information about other potential spouses. Given that information is imperfect, if a wrong choice is made, the result is a divorce. Video dating services, personal advertisements, private investigators, and blood tests are all information services that allow the marriage market to function more efficiently.

Employment and labor markets can also be modeled as markets for information. A prospective employee must provide a resume, references, and information about the level of education and previous work experience to a prospective employer. This information is acquired and used by the employer to determine efficient matches between prospective employees and available jobs. Employment services and employee "headhunters" collect information from prospective employees and employers to make efficient matches. Once employed, information may still be collected on the employee to ensure maximum job performance. Measures of productivity, drug testing, and periodic employment reviews are conducted to improve the firm's efficiency by identifying high-quality employees for promotion and low-quality employees for termination.

Modeling Information Acquisition

Information about the value of a potential spouse, quality of a potential worker, the chance that a hurricane is coming, or the chance that a patient needs an operation has value. Acquiring information increases economic efficiency by increasing one's ability to make "good" decisions. When doctors, lawyers, weather forecasters, or mechanics must make decisions based on imperfect information, there is a greater risk that they may make the wrong decision. If doctors have more information about patients' illnesses, they are more likely to prescribe the correct treatment. If lawyers are better informed about the law, they are more likely to make correct decisions, decreasing the time spent in court, their chances of failure, and perhaps even their clients' bills. If weather forecasters have access to the latest satellite imagery, they are better equipped to make more accurate weather predictions.

Using our example of medical information for doctors, a simple model can be developed that illustrates the benefits and costs of information acquisition. Assume that when a patient arrives at the doctor's office with a set of ailments—high fever, blood in urine, etc.—there is a 50 percent chance that this patient will need an operation and a 50 percent chance that the patient can be cured with a less-expensive drug treatment. Assume that the operation costs $100,000 and the drug treatment costs $1,000. To simplify this example, also assume that given the advanced state of the patient's illness, a decision must be made immediately whether or not this patient will receive an operation. If the risk of not operating is dying, then every doctor and patient will choose the operation even though 50 percent of the operations will not be needed.

Although this example might seem extreme, it illustrates the decisions that medical personnel must make every day, for example, to perform a cesarean section or not, to try this antibiotic or another, to operate or wait, to try this drug treatment or an alternative. In each case, different costs are assigned to possible treatments with different chances that a patient with a given set of symptoms may be cured by a given treatment. A doctor weighs the potential benefit her patient will receive based on the chance the treatment will be effective against the effect on the patient if the treatment is unsuccessful. The doctor's decision is based on the patient's symptoms and any tests that can be performed to help identify his illness.

How much is the information about the patient's illness worth? In the previous example, every patient must spend $100,000 for the operation. However, if a test could be developed to determine which patients could be cured with drug treatment, 50 percent of the operations could be avoided, saving $100,000 times the number of avoided operations minus $1,000 for each drug treatment. If 100 operations were performed each year prior to the invention of this test, then the test would save 100(0.50)($100,000 - 1,000) = $4,950,000.

How much is the information worth to a patient? Again, to simplify this example we must make several assumptions. First, assume that the only cost of the operation or the drug is the financial cost. Also assume that patients and doctors use their expected benefit or costs, in a probabilistic sense, as equivalent to the actual benefits or costs. In other words, a 50 percent chance that the operation is needed and costs $100,000 and a 50 percent chance that the drug is needed and costs $1,000 is equivalent to a cost of 0.50($100,000) + 0.50($1,000), which equals $50,500. This means that patients and doctors are *risk neutral*.

Prior to the creation of a test that would identify the patient's illness, the patient was willing to spend $100,000 on the operation. With the test, the patient now knows that there is a 50 percent chance he may need to spend $100,000 on an operation and a 50 percent chance he may need to spend $1,000 on the drug. On average, the expected expenditure is 0.50($100,000) + 0.50($1,000) + **T,** where **T** is the cost of the test. For the patient to be no worse off than he was before, in a probabilistic sense, this expected payment would have to be less than or equal to the $100,000 he would have to pay without the test. Therefore, if **T** is less than or equal to $49,500, the patient will be no worse off because 0.50($100,000) + 0.50($1,000) + $49,500 = $100,000. Again, assuming 100 operations per year, patients would be willing to pay $49,500(100) = $4,950,000 per year for this test.

In the more general case, let **p** be the probability of an event such as an operation. Then (1 - p) is the probability of that event not occurring. Let C_p be the cost of that event and $C_{(1-p)}$ be the cost of the event not occurring. If **K** is the cost of the action taken without perfect information, then patients are willing to pay as much as **T** for a test as long as equation 8.3 is true.

$$pC_p + (1 - p)C_{(1-p)} + T < K \qquad (8.3)$$

Rarely does a test or other piece of information tell us, with certainty, whether we need an operation or a new carburetor, should take our umbrella to work, or are going to win our legal case. Usually the information increases our knowledge of the chance of different events happening rather than the certainty of them happening. In this case, the willingness-to-pay for the information is the change in the expected value of the result. For example, if access to a legal information database increases the knowledge of an attorney and his ability to be victorious in a case, then the value of that information is the increase in the chance of winning multiplied by whatever the payout might be.

To model this, let **p** be the probability of an attorney winning a legal suit with a value of **S** if he wins. Then **(1 - p)** is the probability of losing with no payout if he loses. The expected payout from the suit equals the probability the attorney wins multiplied by the payout if he wins plus the probability he loses multiplied by his loss. This is shown in equation 8.4.

$$\text{Expected Payout} = pS + (1 - p)0 = pS \qquad (8.4)$$

For example, when similar cases are filed in court by this attorney, he may win 50 percent of the cases and receive a portion of the settlement such that his payout or salary is, on average, $1,000,000. This attorney's expected payout from a similar case is $500,000.

Assume that this attorney now has access to a legal librarian and legal database that can be searched to increase the probability of winning the suit. Let **p*>p** be the probability of winning, given that the legal librarian and database are employed for this case at a cost **T.** The expected payout from the suit is shown in equation 8.5.

$$\text{Expected Payout} = p^*S - T \qquad (8.5)$$

As long as the expected payout from winning the case with the help of the legal librarian is greater than the expected payout from winning the case without the legal librarian, then it is worthwhile to employ the librarian and database, as shown in equation 8.6.

$$p^*S - T \; pS \qquad (8.6)$$

Rearranging terms, this is equivalent to what is shown in equation 8.7.

$$T \; (p^* - p)S \qquad (8.7)$$

In other words, as long as **T**—the cost of the librarian and database—is less than **(p* - p)S**—the difference in the expected payout from winning—it is worth employing the librarian and database. If, for example, the employment of a law librarian and legal database increases the chance of winning a $1,000,000 suit by only 5 percent, the employment has an expected value of $50,000.

The most difficult part about measuring the value of information acquisition is in measuring the parameters of the model: **p*, p,** and **S.** In this example, the law firm could calculate the percentage of cases won with and without the benefit of the law librarian as a proxy for **p*** and **p,** while the average payout in similar cases could be used as a proxy for **S.** Alternatively, one could measure the willingness-to-pay by attorneys for law librarians, law firms' investments in legal libraries and librarians, or the amount of time lawyers or others employed by them spend using legal databases. All of the above would proxy for a lawyer's expected value of access or marginal benefit from this type of information.

Summary

Information reduces uncertainty. Uncertainty can be modeled as a probability that various events might happen. The expected value of an event is the probability weighted average of the value of each event. Information about which event is more likely to happen helps reduce risk.

Sometimes, one side of a market—buyers or sellers—will have more information about what outcome is likely to occur than the other side of the market. Markets with asymmetrical information create a distrust between buyers and sellers that results in the market failing to achieve a socially efficient level of output. To solve the problem, sellers can guarantee product quality and buyers can acquire additional information about the value of the product. Government regulations may also be used to ensure product quality and safety.

Markets for information, by definition, suffer from problems of asymmetrical information, such as moral hazard and adverse selection. However, information markets form to correct for these problems.

The value of the information acquired depends on its usefulness in assessing the chances of different events occurring and the costs or benefits of these different events. The value of health information for a life insurance company provides a benefit of better assessing the longevity of a policyholder at the cost of a doctor's visit. The value of weather information depends on the increased validity of weather forecasts and the costs and benefits incurred from different weather systems. Individual demand or willingness-to-pay for information depends on individual assessment of this information value.

Notes

1. George A. Akerlof, "The Market for 'Lemons': Quality Uncertainty and the Market Mechanism," *Quarterly Journal of Economics* 84, no. 3 (August 1970): 488-500.

2. Jacob Mincer, *Schooling, Experience, and Earnings* (New York: Columbia University Press, 1974); Michael A. Spence, "Job Market Signaling," *Quarterly Journal of Economics* 83, no. 3 (August 1973): 355-74.

Chapter 9

Commodity or Public Good

A frequent debate in information and library science is about whether information should be viewed as a commodity or a public good. The commodity model suggests that information should be bought and sold in a market and, like other commodities, the market price would determine which suppliers are cost-efficient enough to sell it and which consumers receive sufficient value to pay for it. In the public good model, information can and should be shared among many consumers while collecting sufficient revenue to cover the cost of production.

Information can be modeled as both a commodity and a public good. When buyers and sellers exchange information services or products in markets, information is a private good or commodity. Books sold at a bookstore, newspapers sold on the street corner, computer software for individual use, individual journal subscriptions, and individual phone use are all examples of information goods or services as commodities. In each case, the service or good provides benefit to a single consumer, who pays for the supply of that service or good.

Information services or products can also be public goods. Books sold to libraries, newspapers shared by co-workers, computer software networked among several work stations, a library journal subscription, and a telephone network are all examples of information goods or services as public goods. In these examples there are several individuals who benefit from the consumption of the same good. Several patrons can use the same book or journal from the library over the course of a year. Several people can simultaneously use computer software on a network. Everyone uses the same telephone network.

The same good or service can be modeled as both a public and a private good. The correct choice of modeling depends on the economic analysis to be done. The public good model examines the collective benefit of a good or service. The decisions of how to finance the good, who should pay for it, and how much each individual should pay will be determined by the collective benefit of several individuals. The private good model assumes that a single individual receives the benefit from the consumption of a good or service. Production of the good is typically financed by individual consumers purchasing individual units of the good for their private benefit. The level of output in the market is determined by the demand and supply of the good.

The "commodity" or "private good" model of information goods or services is a model in which individuals benefit from their consumption and, at times, expect to pay for the benefits they receive in the same way they purchase other private goods. The "public good" or "social good" model of information goods and services is a model in which there is a collective benefit that consumers or individuals receive from a good or service. The choice of model—public good or commodity—can be illustrated by examining the market for books purchased by individuals and libraries and the market for computer software and research and development.

Market for Books and Journals

The market for books and journals has both private good and public good characteristics. The purchase of books and journals by faculty, students, libraries, or other consumers should be modeled as a private good. Each buyer weighs the benefits that arise from his purchase against the cost of the book or journal. In the case of individual consumers, the benefit from purchasing a book or journal is received by the consumer. Although the library benefit is delivered to many patrons, the purchase is made by a single agent—an acquisitions librarian—who must weigh the benefits to all potential users. As with an individual consumer, the benefits received by library patrons must exceed the book or journal's purchase price. Figure 9.1 illustrates the market for books.

The demand for books can be divided between library and non-library consumers. Non-library purchases of books include books sold at retail outlets and ordered from publishers. Non-library purchases represent over 95 percent of the market for books. Libraries represent less than 5 percent of the total market for books, but because of their higher benefits from books, based on the collective benefits of their patrons, the library demand is concentrated in the upper range of the market demand curve.

For simplicity, Figure 9.1 assumes that publishers charge each consumer the same price for a book. Although it over-generalizes the market for books, its intent is to illustrate how the private market for books functions rather than to focus on a particular segment of this market.

The supply curve in Figure 9.1 is upward sloping. The figure does not represent the costs of a single publisher in making books; rather, it represents the supply of books by all publishers. The upward-sloping supply curve means that an increase in the average price of a book will result in more publishers offering more books for sale.

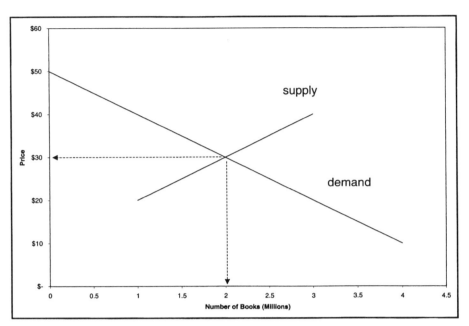

Figure 9.1. Market for Books.

In Figure 9.1, the equilibrium quantity of books sold is 2 million. If the demand curve accurately reflects the marginal benefit from books, then 2 million is also the economically efficient or pareto optimum number of books. For individual consumers of books, the demand curve will accurately represent the private marginal benefit or willingness-to-pay for books. However, it is unclear whether the demand for books by libraries accurately reflects the marginal benefit library patrons receive from books. For the library demand to accurately reflect patron marginal benefits, acquisitions librarians must be able to accurately measure or estimate the value of their library books to patrons. The difficulty of estimating this value to patrons is illustrated in Figure 9.2.

Figure 9.2 shows the public good demand or public good marginal benefit curve for books in a hypothetical public library. The sum of the marginal benefits of individual patrons who use the library equals the marginal benefit or public good demand curve for books in the library. In Figure 9.2 the 30,000th book purchased by the public library has a marginal benefit of $40. This $40 marginal benefit might represent the use of a book by four patrons, each of which receives $10 in benefit from that particular book.

The marginal cost of a book for the library equals the market equilibrium price, $30 in Figure 9.1. For simplicity we have assumed that the cost of cataloguing the book is trivial. Therefore, the economically efficient number of books purchased by the public library is 40,000, where the marginal benefit of a book equals the marginal cost to the library.

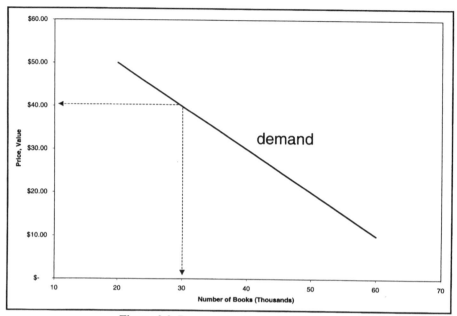

Figure 9.2. Demand for Books by Library.

Each library will have a similar public good demand or marginal benefit curve for books. If librarians can accurately predict their patrons' marginal benefit from books, then the actual demand or willingness-to-pay for books by libraries will reflect the public good demand or marginal benefit that patrons receive from the libraries. An estimate of the value of books to patrons can come from library patron surveys, user data, and local referendums on public library funding.

It is unlikely that librarians will have full information about their patrons' marginal benefit and that voters for public library funding and patrons are the same group and share common preferences. If, for example, voters under-represent the marginal benefit library patrons receive from the public library, the library budget approved by voters will be less than the marginal benefit patrons receive from the library. In this case, the number of books purchased by the library will be less than the socially efficient level. If the number of books the library purchases at $30 is less than 40,000, the demand for books in Figure 9.1 will be less than the marginal benefit of book purchases. The number of books purchased will be less than 2 million (see Figure 9.3).

In Figure 9.3, **Q** books are purchased, which is less than the economically efficient level of books, 2 million. Although the demand for books by individual consumers accurately reflects the marginal benefit they receive from books, the library demand under-represents the marginal benefit patrons receive from books and, therefore, fewer books are purchased. Books between **Q** and 2 million have a marginal benefit, to library patrons, which is greater than the marginal cost of producing these books, and, as a result, deadweight loss or economic inefficiency is produced. This deadweight loss is represented by the shaded area in Figure 9.3.

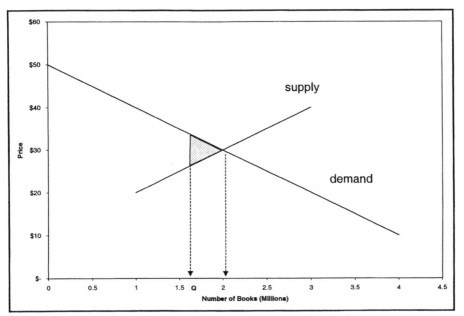

Figure 9.3. Deadweight Loss in Market for Books.

With public goods, if the collective financing mechanism does not accurately reflect the marginal benefit to consumers, there will be economic inefficiency. In other words, if voters, acquisitions librarians, library directors, or patrons are unable to translate patrons' marginal benefits into library financing and purchasing policy, the number of books purchased will be less than the economically efficient level. As with most public goods, information services and products that require the government to provide financing or must rely on voluntary contributions for financing may not be efficiently provided. This underscores the importance of the need for library directors and voters to gain information about the use and worth of the local library. Patron surveys, voter education, and analysis of library-use patterns are all effective methods of gathering information that can be used to justify financing for the local library.

Information Markets

Not all information goods and services that are public goods rely on government financing. Movies, video rentals, credit reports, and news in a newspaper are all public goods financed through sales. In each example, more than one consumer enjoys the same good or service. The same movie is consumed by everyone who purchases a ticket or rents the video to see it. Your credit record is a public good for all potential lenders to access, for a fee. The news in a newspaper is read by many individuals simultaneously. Individual purchases of the newspaper and the advertising revenue pay for the writers, editors, and printers of the newspaper.

The market for software also has public and private good characteristics. Individuals purchase copies of the software, which finances the creativity and innovation required to produce it. The "intellectual property" of the research and development that goes into producing a software program is a public good for all future users of the software.

Figure 9.4 illustrates the market for a hypothetical software program. Given the high fixed costs of developing software and lower marginal cost of producing an additional copy of it, the average cost curve for copies of a program is downward sloping. The demand for this software program comes from new academic and business users, users of competing programs, and users of earlier versions of the software.

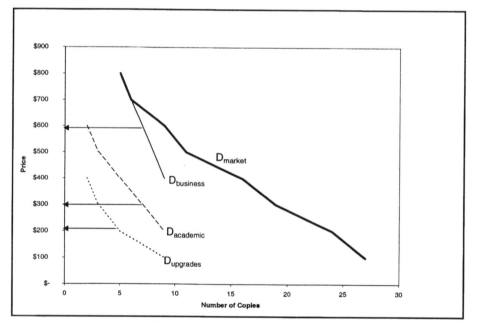

Figure 9.4. Market for Software.

Manufacturers of computer software can segment the demand for computer software and charge a different price to each segment. Typically, business users have a greater demand for the latest version of computer programs and, without an academic affiliation, must pay a higher price for a copy. Academic users, with more limited resources and lower marginal benefits, pay a lower price than business users. Note that this does not exclude the possibility that some academic users may receive a higher marginal benefit from the software than some business users; it only means that a larger fraction of business users are willing to pay more for the software than a majority of academic users. Finally, users of competing programs or of earlier versions have a lower willingness-to-pay for an upgrade because they can simply continue to use the old program. Therefore, those purchasing upgrades are given a lower price.

The inventor of a particular word processing program maximizes profit by segmenting the market among these three groups of consumers. The copyright on the program enables the inventor to make revenues in excess of marginal costs, which can then be used to cover the costs of creative activity or innovation. This profit also motivates software creators and manufacturers to improve their products through additional research and development.

The marginal benefit to software manufacturers of research and development in a product is the sum of the expected revenue from individual consumers. In other words, research and development is a public good in that individual marginal benefit from an upgraded computer program is represented by the profit that a software corporation might receive from the upgrade. Figure 9.5 illustrates this public good characteristic of research and development.

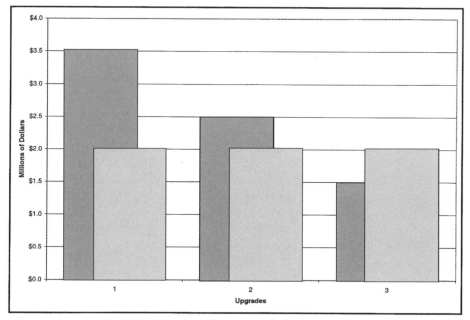

Figure 9.5. Expected Revenue and Cost of Upgrades.

In Figure 9.5, the demand for research and development in the first version of this software program is the sum of the expected revenue from each copy sold. As additional versions are created, fewer users are willing to upgrade their program or switch from other word processing programs. As a result, each successive upgrade has a lower level of revenue per unit and a lower expected total profit. This effect depends on the amount of time between releases of the new software.

The first two upgrades have an expected revenue greater than their costs and are, therefore, economically efficient investments. However, the third upgrade does not produce sufficient profit to cover its cost. In a few years, as consumer tastes change, personal computers improve, or more consumers purchase personal computers, the expected profit from additional upgrades may increase and exceed the cost of research and development of the third upgrade. The timing of new releases of computer software is critical. Software manufacturers closely watch the release of new computer hardware, processors, and operating systems to determine when investments should be made in new upgrades of existing programs.

Research and development is a public good financed by expected profits on sales. However, this is possible only if creators or inventors can get a return on their good or service. Copyright and patent laws create an exclusionary mechanism that finances information goods and services that are public goods.

As the previous example illustrates, modeling information goods or services as public goods does not imply that government financing is the most efficient way to pay for the good. Many information services and products that are public goods are financed through user fees, donations, and advertising. Research and development, movies, and cable broadcasts are financed using exclusionary user fees. Public television stations are financed using a combination of government funding and donations, while commercial television is financed using advertising revenues.

Likewise, modeling an information good or service as a private good does not imply that user fees or prices are the most efficient mechanism for finance. Many information goods and services that might logically be modeled as private goods are efficiently financed through taxes, donations, and advertising. Public library reference services, magazines, and education can be modeled as private goods, yet are financed in a variety of ways. Reference librarians are asked questions by individual patrons who might otherwise be charged user fees for the information received. Library reference services are paid by tax revenues and donations. In this case, the cost of imposing and collecting user fees may outweigh the value of the service, making user fees an inefficient method of financing. Magazines are financed by sales and advertising revenues, while education is financed by tuition, donations, and government funding.

Summary

Information goods and services can be modeled as public and private goods. The choice of model depends on the economic analysis to be done. If the good or service provides a collective benefit to more than one consumer, it should be modeled as a public good. If the good or service provides a private benefit to individual consumers, it should be modeled as a private good or commodity.

All information goods can be modeled as public goods. Information typically benefits more than one consumer. News, entertainment, scholarship, and research and development are all information goods that are produced with the intent of providing benefit to more than one consumer. However, the delivery mechanism of information is typically a private good or commodity. Compact disks, books, magazines, and newspapers are intended to be purchased by one individual, making the distribution mechanism a private good. On the Internet, a networked environment, the distribution of the information is to individuals but within the public good model. Each individual is consuming the same information simultaneously.

In either case, there are several potential methods of financing the good or service. Collective mechanisms such as tax revenues and donations are typically used to finance public goods. However, advertising revenues and exclusionary user fees can also be used to finance public goods. Private information goods and services may also be financed by user fees, advertising revenues, taxes, and donations.

Chapter 10

Pricing

Prices serve a dual purpose: to allocate the supply of goods and services and to finance the production of these goods and services. When a good or service is purchased, the role of the price to finance the good is the role we are most familiar with. Suppliers collect revenue through the sale of a good and use the revenue to cover costs and make a profit. To the publishers of books, journals, newspapers, and software and to any other commercial information provider, the primary purpose of sales is to pay for costs and generate profits. The price paid for a computer software program is used to pay for the cost of the floppy disks and instruction manual, to compensate authors for their intellectual property, and to compensate the owners of the company for their creativity and management skills. Movie tickets, video rental charges, telephone charges, and the price of a newspaper are all user fees collected to finance the production of these goods and services.

Revenues collected from user fees are also used to finance output in the nonprofit and government sectors. In a library, photocopy revenues are used to purchase paper and toner and to lease the photocopy machine; revenues collected from overdue library fines can be used to purchase more books. Governments may charge for genealogical records, driver records, or other government documents. These fees finance government expenses including the cost of providing the information.

Prices as allocation mechanisms determine who can purchase certain goods and services. At a given price, only those consumers who receive a benefit from the good greater than the price will purchase it. This ensures that consumers with the most benefit from a good will receive it and that consumers do not abuse or take for granted their consumption of a good. There are many examples of goods

113

and services that, if given away, consumers would abuse. For example, if the photocopy machines in academic libraries were free, you would not be surprised to find undergraduate students making copies of their faces simply to entertain themselves. The New York State Library does not charge overdue book fines. As a result, many patrons do not return borrowed books. For each patron who does not return a book, the library sends out countless overdue notices. The absence of a price or fee for extra use results in these patrons' inconsiderate behavior to others who want to use overdue materials. Most libraries charge overdue book fines to prevent this problem.

In the case of information goods and services, a price's allocation role and the financing role frequently conflict. To finance the good or service, the price charged must be at least equal to the average cost of producing the good for the consumer. Only then will sufficient revenues be collected from each consumer to cover the cost of producing the good. However, the allocative function of user fees requires setting a price equal to the marginal or additional cost of providing the good, to achieve economic efficiency. Many information goods have low or no marginal costs. Books, journals, and computer software all have high first-copy or fixed costs but lower marginal costs for additional copies. Providing information on the Internet has no marginal cost of reproduction and delivery. There is no additional cost of one more user accessing a given web site. In this case, marginal cost pricing would require a price of zero, although this would not provide sufficient revenue to cover the costs of production.

This chapter examines the allocative and financing roles of user fees for information goods and services. The first two sections of this chapter examine the allocative function of prices, focusing on setting price to achieve an economically or socially efficient allocation while disregarding the need for revenues. This is the traditional microeconomic analysis of pricing, which does not adequately explain the role of prices for information goods. This chapter also examines Ramsey prices, which balance the need to collect revenues and maintain economic efficiency while charging all consumers the same price. The last section of this chapter examines value-based prices that, if consumer value can be determined, enable organizations to collect sufficient revenue to cover costs and attain economic efficiency. The economics of information relies on value-based pricing to achieve economic efficiency.

User Fees as Allocation Tools

Whether user fees are charged for photocopying, library information, or government information, prices equal to marginal costs maximize the benefit to consumers or patrons of the cost of producing the information. The efficiency of marginal cost pricing is illustrated in Figure 10.1, which shows the demand, or marginal benefit and marginal cost, of photocopying in an academic library.

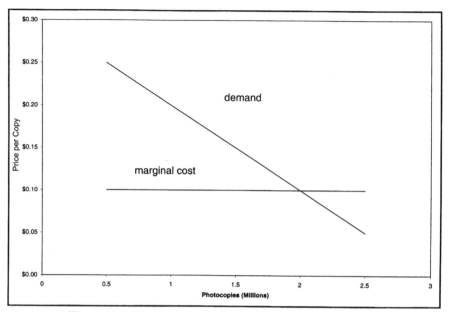

Figure 10.1. Marginal Cost Pricing of Library Photocopying.

In Figure 10.1, the marginal cost of a photocopy is $0.10. These are costs associated with the consumer's use of the copier but not the fixed costs incurred regardless of any consumer's level of use. Marginal costs include the cost of paper, toner, and any employee time needed for assistance. Fixed costs include the annual leasing or replacement cost of the photocopy machine.

Given the marginal cost and marginal benefit as illustrated in Figure 10.1, the optimal price of a photocopy is $0.10. At this price, the level of photocopying, 2 million copies, is such that the marginal benefit from an additional photocopy equals the marginal cost. If the price were set below $0.10, too many copies would be made. At prices less than $0.10, copies would be made at a marginal cost greater than the marginal benefit. If the price were set above $0.10, too few copies would be made and copies could be made at a marginal benefit greater than the marginal cost. At any price other than $0.10, an inefficient number of copies will be made.

Figure 10.2 shows the inefficiency that results if the price of a photocopy is $0.20. At that price, only 1 million photocopies are made. However, the 1 millionth photocopy provides a marginal benefit of $0.20, which is greater than the marginal cost of $0.10 to produce it. In fact, all copies between the 1 millionth copy and the 2 millionth copy provide benefits to consumers that exceed the additional cost of the copy. A price of $0.20 prevents these additional copies from being made and denies consumers the net benefit from them. The inefficiency or deadweight loss resulting from a price of $0.20 per copy is represented by the shaded area in Figure 10.2.

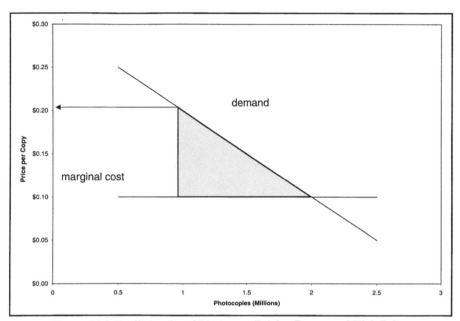

Figure 10.2. Inefficiencies of Photocopy Pricing Because of High Price.

Figure 10.3 illustrates what would happen if the price of a copy were only $0.05. In this case, photocopies would be made that have a marginal benefit less than the marginal cost of producing them. At $0.05 a copy, the 2.5 millionth copy has a marginal benefit of $0.05 to the patron but a marginal cost of paper and toner of $0.10 to the library. The copies in excess of 2 million each have a benefit less than the costs incurred from making these copies. By making these copies in excess of 2 million, suppliers must pay more than the benefit of the copies. The inefficiency or deadweight loss in this case is represented by the shaded area in Figure 10.3.

Only a price of $0.10 will ensure that all photocopying with a marginal benefit greater than $0.10 will be done, while copying with a marginal benefit of less than $0.10 will not. Therefore, $0.10 is the price that results in economic efficiency in this market.

Charging $0.10 for a photocopy also covers the marginal costs in this example. Revenues received from patrons pay for paper, toner, and labor associated with the photocopy machine. This is the financing mechanism of the price. Each copy results in exactly the marginal cost of providing it to the patron. However, with a charge of $0.10, the fixed costs of leasing or purchasing the photocopier are not covered.

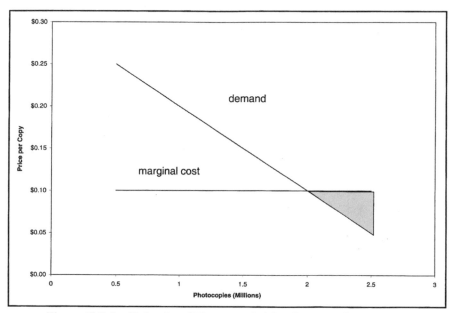

Figure 10.3. Inefficiencies of Photocopy Pricing Because of Low Price.

Marginal Cost of Pricing

Charging user fees is not cost-free. There is a cost associated with setting prices and collecting revenue. Collecting revenue for photocopying requires adding Vendacard or coin attachments to the photocopy machine, installing and stocking Vendacard dispensing machines, plus collecting the money. Charging user fees for library services, access to government information, or any other service requires recording and collecting fees that, for individual transactions, can add a significant cost in addition to the cost of producing and providing the information.

Because many information products have low marginal costs of production, the cost of pricing may not make it worthwhile to implement user fees. For example, the marginal cost of borrowing a book from the library is the few seconds that the librarian must service and record your request. The fixed costs of the book have already been incurred by the library and should not be included in the marginal cost of borrowing. Imposing user fees on patrons equal to the marginal cost of borrowing would raise little revenue and imposes additional costs on the library of collecting fees and maintaining records of this revenue. Not imposing a user fee results in some deadweight loss. Because the book is free to borrow for a limited time, there will be some patrons who receive a benefit less than the marginal cost of borrowing the book and there will be borrowing in excess of the economically efficient level. However, the costs of imposing user fees would probably be greater than the deadweight loss avoided. The cost of implementing a user fee would outweigh the benefit of marginal cost pricing.

Information sources such as photocopying, reading magazines in a store, database searching, or searching CDs in the library may have marginal costs sufficiently low that implementing user fees would not be economically efficient. Figure 10.4 illustrates this using the example of library patrons.

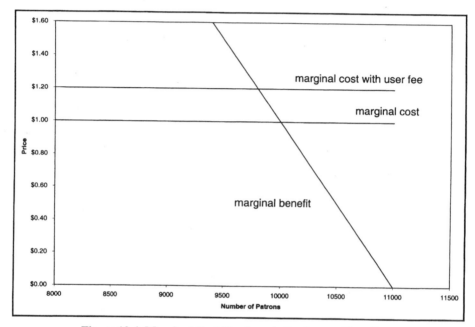

Figure 10.4. Marginal Cost Too Low to Implement User Fees.

Figure 10.4 models the private demand for library services by patrons. It shows the marginal benefit to patrons of using the library and the marginal cost of servicing them. The marginal cost of servicing a patron is the cost of time and effort of the librarian to help the patron and reshelve the patron's returned books. If the librarian spends a total of five minutes on this patron's transaction and is paid $12 per hour, then the marginal cost of a patron's use of the library is $1.00.

Not charging a user fee invites patrons to use the library who have a marginal benefit from library use less than the marginal cost of servicing them. These are the patrons from 10,000 to 11,000 in Figure 10.4. The cost of servicing them is the marginal cost ($1.00) multiplied by the number of extra patrons (1,000), which equals $1,000. The benefit these patrons receive from using the library is the area under the marginal benefit curve from 10,000 to 11,000. This area equals 0.5($1.00)(1,000), or $500. The resulting deadweight loss is equal to $500 ($1,000 - $500) or the amount when costs of servicing these patrons exceed the benefit they receive from using the library.

To eliminate this deadweight loss, a user fee equal to the marginal cost could be charged to all patrons. However, charging patrons for using the library costs money. Assume each financial transaction costs an additional one minute of the librarian's time. Then the library's cost of charging a fee is $0.20 per patron (1/60 of an hour times $12 per hour). If a user fee is implemented, the new marginal cost of patron use is at $1.20 in Figure 10.4—the cost of the patron using the library plus the cost of charging the patron a user fee.

Charging patrons $1.20 per use of the library will eliminate the deadweight loss of $500, because patrons who benefit less than $1.20 will no longer use the library. However, this increase in the marginal cost reduces patron-consumer surplus. The reduction in patron-consumer surplus equals the consumer surplus patrons would have received without a charge but now must give up in the form of a fee to pay for the marginal costs of charging. In Figure 10.4, the consumer surplus loss is approximately $0.20 times 10,000 patrons, which equals $2,000. Therefore, patrons and the library will lose more in increased costs or lost consumer surplus ($2,000) than they will gain by eliminating the deadweight loss of patrons who receive less benefit from the library than the cost of servicing them ($500).

Whether to charge user fees depends on the elasticity of demand. The less elastic patrons are to user fees, the less deadweight loss is eliminated with charging. In Figure 10.5, **MB'** is a more elastic marginal benefit curve than **MB**. This means that patrons are more responsive to changes in the cost of using the library and less likely to use the library if the cost of using it increases. This may be true of small libraries with a limited number of patrons who are very sensitive to charging a user fee, or libraries located near bookstores where patrons are just as willing to purchase books at the bookstore as they are to use the library, or a branch library located in a shopping mall where many patrons might simply be using the library's restroom rather than checking out books.

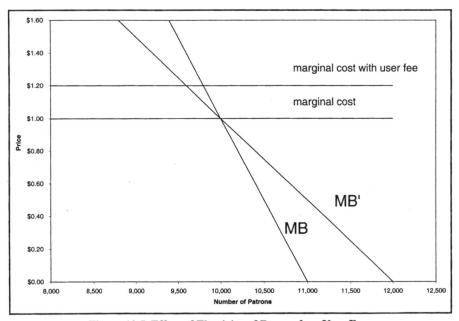

Figure 10.5. Effect of Elasticity of Demand on User Fees.

With a more elastic demand curve for library services, the deadweight loss resulting from not charging is greater than with a less elastic curve. Not charging patrons for using library services encourages a larger number of patrons who have a marginal benefit of service less than the marginal cost to use the library. This implies that it is more likely that economic efficiency will be improved by charging user fees when the demand for information services is more elastic.

The efficiency of implementing user fees also depends on the marginal cost of charging. The lower the marginal cost of charging, the lower the loss in consumer surplus from implementing charges. This is illustrated in Figure 10.6.

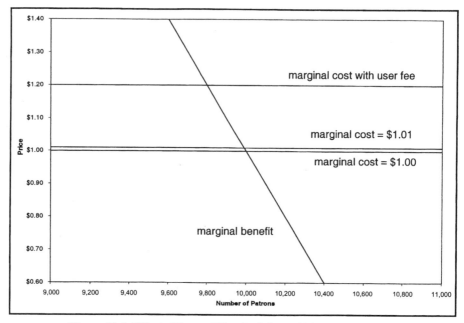

Figure 10.6. Effect of Lower Marginal Cost of Library User Fees.

In Figure 10.6, the marginal cost of charging is lowered from $0.20 to $0.01 per patron. This can happen if there is a new electronic system available that makes charging user fees less costly. The lost consumer surplus from charging decreases from approximately $2,000 to $100. In this case, because the marginal cost of charging patrons, $100, is less than the deadweight loss from not charging, $500, user fees improve economic efficiency by $400.

Technological advances frequently result in a lower cost of charging. New cash registers and bar coding decrease the cost of charging in grocery stores, and improvements in scanning technology have decreased the cost of charging drivers on toll roads. As these technological advances have decreased the costs of charging, they have also decreased the consumer surplus loss when user fees are implemented. As a result, technological advances have increased the chance that implementing user fees for information goods and services might improve economic efficiency.

The technological advances of the Internet may decrease the efficiency of charging user fees on the World Wide Web. Instant access to information in a networked environment lowers the marginal cost of access to 0. With a 0 marginal cost of reproduction, the deadweight loss from not charging a user fee would be 0. User fees, regardless of how small, will increase the cost of access on the Internet and decrease consumer surplus. Therefore it would be more economically efficient to not charge user access fees for online information.

Financing Information Goods: Ramsey Prices

Prices serve not only to allocate resources but also to finance goods and services. Revenues collected from photocopiers go toward purchasing photocopier supplies, overdue book fees are used to finance library operations, and admission charges for movies finance the movie production and theater expenses. Any time user fees are charged, the revenues collected from these fees may or may not cover the cost of the service. When costs exceed revenues, financing from the sale of other goods, taxes, or donations must be used to cover costs. When revenues exceed costs, there is a profit which, at commercial firms, is used to reward employees, managers, or owners. In the public and nonprofit sectors, excess revenues are used to reward employees or finance other goods.

Library directors or government administrators must determine what prices to charge, not only to efficiently supply individual goods and services, but also to finance the provision of goods and services for which sufficient revenues are not collected. For example, it may be worthwhile for the library director to charge a price for photocopying above the marginal cost and use surplus revenues to finance the purchase of more books, journals, or other worthy expenditures. Some nonprofit organizations sell magazines and other goods at a profit and use these revenues to finance other services. Universities use surplus tuition revenues to finance computer services for which students and faculty are not charged. In each example, an organization has the ability to price above cost when selling one good and use these surplus revenues to cross-subsidize the production of another good. Prices are used to pay for the production of goods and services which, for various reasons, cannot cover their costs but should be provided. How optimal prices are chosen under these circumstances is illustrated in Figure 10.7.

Figure 10.7 represents the market for photocopying in a library. Assume that the cost of implementing user fees is minimal so that we do not have to consider the increase in marginal cost. This is a reasonable assumption if there is an existing fee for photocopying and increasing this fee will have little effect on the cost of collecting additional revenues. According to Figure 10.7, the economically efficient price to charge for photocopying is $0.10 per copy, at which 2 million copies would be made. If a price of $0.15 per copy were charged, there would be a decrease in photocopying to 1.8 million copies and a deadweight loss equal to the value of the decrease in photocopying, which equals $5,000 (one-half of the price increase of $0.05 times the quantity decrease of 200,000).

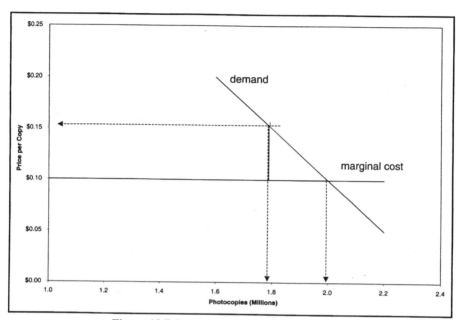

Figure 10.7. Pricing of Library Photocopying.

This pricing policy produces deadweight loss and also yields revenues above marginal cost. Revenues net of marginal costs equal the difference between $0.10 and $0.15 multiplied by the number of photocopies, 1.8 million. Net revenues equal $90,000. In total, patrons lose $95,000 in consumer surplus from the price increase, with $90,000 going to the library as profit and $5,000 lost as a result of the decrease in photocopying.

Economic efficiency depends on the value of the use of this additional revenue. Revenues could go toward hiring an additional reference worker, buying additional books or journals, or paying for capital improvements or for other fixed costs at the library. For example, if these revenues go to providing 10 additional networked computing stations, the net marginal benefit of these workstations may be greater than the deadweight loss produced from the higher photocopy price. Figure 10.8 shows the marginal benefit and marginal cost of additional networked personal computers at this library. If the library budget presently only allows for the employment of 40 workstations, but an additional 10 computers provide an additional annual benefit of $120,000 at a cost of $90,000, then library patrons will receive a net marginal benefit of $30,000 from the computers. Library patrons will actually be better off if the price of photocopying is increased to pay for the additional computers. Patrons lose $95,000 in consumer surplus but gain $120,000 in benefit from the additional reference worker. In other words, library patrons "purchase" $30,000 in net benefits at a cost of $5,000 in deadweight loss from their photocopying. On net, patrons gain $25,000 after the price of photocopying is increased to pay for additional networked computers.

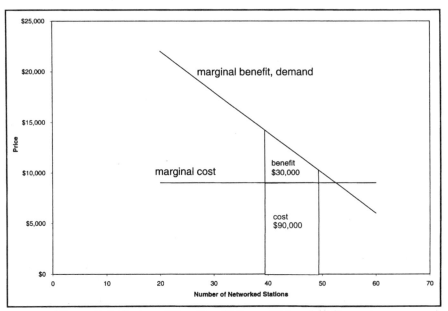

Figure 10.8. Costs and Benefits of Library Networked Computers.

Ramsey prices are a set of optimal prices above marginal cost that provide financing to supply goods and services.[1] Prices above marginal cost that produce deadweight loss in one market are used to finance the production of other goods and services that have a benefit in excess of the deadweight loss. The deadweight loss resulting from increasing the price of photocopying, overdue book fines, or user fees for acquiring government information must be compared to the value of the services purchased with surplus revenues. Economic efficiency is increased when the deadweight loss of increasing the price on one good or service is less than the net benefit produced from the use of the additional revenue.

Financing Information Goods: Value-Based Prices

Computer software manufacturers will set different prices for different consumers for the same software. The same software program may be sold to business consumers, academic consumers, and the home personal computer user for different prices. Typically business consumers pay more and academic consumers receive a discount on the standard price for software. Companies willing to purchase a license for several users will receive a discount for each user or a site license for a lower cost per user than purchasing an equal number of individual licenses. Subscriptions to academic journals also have different prices for different types of consumers for the same journal. Academic libraries will pay more for a journal subscription than a faculty member will, and student subscriptions usually cost less than faculty subscriptions.

These are examples of value-based pricing. Value-based prices are based on the value that consumers receive from a good. The more value a consumer receives from a good, the more she is willing to pay for it and, subsequently, the higher the price she is charged. Value-based pricing solves the problem of financing information goods when marginal cost pricing does not provide sufficient revenue to cover the fixed cost of producing an information good. Prices based on the value of a good to the consumer will provide revenue equal to the benefit from a good. As long as the benefit of consuming a good is greater than the cost, the revenue should be sufficient to provide financing for production.

Consider the example of producing a computer software program. Assume that the development cost for the program is $1 million. The marginal cost of producing additional copies of the program on CD may be $1.00 per copy. In this case, marginal cost pricing will never produce sufficient revenues to cover the cost of developing this software. The hypothetical demand for this software is shown in Table 10.1.

Table 10.1
Sector Demand and Revenue for Computer Software

	Market		Sector Demand			Sector Revenue		
Price	Demand	Revenue	Business	Home	Academic	Business	Home	Academic
$600	1,350	$810,000	1,000	300	50	$600,000	$180,000	$30,000
$500	1,900	$950,000	1,400	400	100	$700,000	$200,000	$50,000
$400	2,450	$980,000	1,700	500	250	$680,000	$200,000	$100,000
$300	3,150	$945,000	1,900	750	500	$570,000	$225,000	$150,000
$200	4,500	$900,000	2,000	1,500	1,000	$400,000	$300,000	$200,000
$100	6,900	$690,000	2,100	2,700	2,100	$210,000	$270,000	$210,000
$50	10,700	$535,000	2,200	5,000	3,500	$110,000	$250,000	$175,000

If the producer of this software charges a single price for all consumers, then the revenue-maximizing price is $400 per copy, which results in $980,000 in revenue. This falls short of the $1 million in costs to produce this software. However, if the producer charges different prices to the different market segments based on the value that each sector places on this software, it is possible to cover the costs of development. In this case the producer can charge a price of $500 for the business version and generate $700,000 in revenue; charge $200 to home users and generate $300,000 in revenue; and charge $100 to academic users and generate $210,000 in revenue, for a total of $1,210,000. Only value-based pricing results in sufficient revenue to cover the costs of production.

Value-based pricing may still result in deadweight loss in this market. There are still business, home, and academic consumers that would receive a benefit from this software but are not willing to purchase it at the price charged to their market sector. For example, at a price of $500, an additional 800 business consumers are willing to pay between $50 and $499 for the software. This value is lost to society unless these business consumers can be charged a price equal to their value. A different price for each business, home, and academic user would have to be charged in order to sell a copy of the software to each consumer that received value from it, while at the same time collecting sufficient revenue to cover costs.

Summary

The allocation role of prices requires that prices be set equal to marginal costs to achieve economic efficiency. Prices above or below marginal costs will result in deadweight loss. If prices are less than marginal costs, some units will be consumed at a cost higher than the benefit consumers receive from them. If prices are greater than marginal costs, units that have benefits greater than their costs will not be purchased.

A more complete analysis of user fees in information markets must also include the marginal cost of implementing prices and the potential use of surplus revenues. The cost of pricing may imply that implementing user fees for some information goods and services imposes a greater cost on consumers than the decrease in deadweight loss from not charging user fees. Prices above marginal cost may result in a more efficient level of overall service as long as the value of services provided with excess revenues exceeds the deadweight loss incurred. User-fee financing requires a complete analysis of all related goods and services to determine the optimal user fee for any given good or service.

With information goods, marginal cost pricing typically does not provide sufficient revenue to cover costs. Government and nonprofit organizations may use Ramsey prices to provide sufficient revenues. Value-based pricing and segmenting markets may also provide sufficient revenue to cover costs. Value-based pricing also enables firms to maximize profits by collecting more revenue in each market segment than is possible with a single price for all consumers. Different prices for the same product in different countries, for different consumer types, or for different businesses are examples of value-based pricing.

Notes

1. Frank P. Ramsey, "A Contribution to the Theory of Taxation," *Economic Journal* (1927): 47-61.

Chapter 11

Time

Many information goods and services take time to consume. Going to a movie, reading a book, attending a lecture, or making a telephone call are activities that require an investment of time. The price or financial cost of these goods is only a small part of the full economic cost or opportunity cost of consuming them. The opportunity cost of these goods is the purchase price or fee plus the value of time spent consuming them. The opportunity cost of a movie or a lecture is the ticket price or tuition paid plus the value of the time spent traveling to and watching the movie or listening to the lecture. The opportunity cost of a book is the price of the book plus the value of the time spent reading it. The opportunity cost of a telephone call is the financial cost of the call plus the value of the time spent talking.

Demand or cost-benefit analysis of these markets must include the value of time spent on consumption to reflect accurately the value of these goods and the willingness of patrons, users, or consumers to pay for them. Using only the financial price paid for these goods or services undervalues the benefit consumers receive from them and the cost consumers incur. When commercial firms analyze the demand for time-intensive goods and services, the consumers' value of the time spent acquiring these goods is an important factor in the analysis. For example, a three-hour movie epic may be of sufficient quality to sell more movie tickets; however, when analyzing demand for film epics, film studios consider the patron's willingness to spend time to view the movie. Shorter films require less viewing time. Demand analysis of books, direct marketing, and television ads includes a valuation of consumer time. The optimal length of new books, amount of information sent via direct marketing, or length of a television ad are all influenced by the value of time of potential consumers.

Measuring the value of time is also important in cost-benefit analyses of information goods and services provided by government and nonprofit organizations. Analyses of the benefits and costs of providing books and journals to library patrons, tax forms and other government-provided information to taxpayers, and computer systems for employees require an assessment of the value of time spent using these goods. The opportunity cost of books and journals in a library must include the value of the time spent by patrons reading them. However, there may also be the economic benefit of time saved by patrons, who can get information immediately from the library rather than waiting for a book or journal article to be delivered to them. The opportunity cost of a tax form involves the government's printing and shipping costs as well as the value of time spent by taxpayers filling out the forms. Finally, the opportunity cost of computing systems depends on the processing speed of each system.

New technology may decrease the amount of time spent using information goods or services. For example, a personal computer with a next generation processor is faster than one with an older processor. When making a decision to purchase the faster computer, one must consider not only the financial difference between the two computers but also the value of the time it takes to run software using the two different processors. Most libraries now have electronic catalogs to speed patron searching of the library's holdings, a significant time savings compared to the old card catalogs. Libraries also give patrons access to information on compact disks, which speed the research process compared to comparable print resources.

Failure to include the value of time to users in a cost-benefit analysis can result in serious mistakes in the valuation of particular information systems or services. For example, many libraries now rely extensively on interlibrary loan to provide patrons with access to journals the library does not subscribe to. Libraries frequently save money by canceling underused journal subscriptions and providing them to patrons via interlibrary loan. However, a complete cost analysis of these alternative methods of access must include the value of the time spent by patrons waiting for the articles to be delivered via interlibrary loan.

Measuring the Value of Time

The value of time spent on one activity is the value or cost of forgone opportunities during that time. For example, if you get paid $8.50 per hour and decide to take the last three hours of the afternoon off from work to go to the movies, you will have foregone $25.50 in potential earnings. Whenever you take off from work to consume a good, the time spent in consumption can simply be valued as the income you would have earned had you stayed at work.

The most basic and most frequently used method of measuring the value of time is to use an individual's hourly wage. An attorney may charge clients $150 per hour. If he chooses to spend an hour at lunch instead of an hour at the office with a client, he loses $150. If you make $20 per hour as an academic librarian and choose to "spend" an hour of your time reading a book, we can estimate the value of the time as $20. Likewise, if you work as a cashier and make $6 per hour and choose to spend an hour shopping, you are forgoing $6 in wages.

Time spent away from work during the evenings and weekends may also be valued at an individual's wage rate. It may be somewhat unrealistic to think that everyone can simply work an extra hour and make an extra $6 or $150, particularly salaried employees who do not get paid by the hour; however, many employees can choose to work additional hours during evenings and weekends. Some employees may work extra hours to increase their job skills or their employer's opinion of them, thereby hoping to be promoted and increase their salary. In any case, using an individual's wage rate is a good approximation of the value of an hour to the employee and an approximation of his hourly value to his employer.

Measuring Opportunity Costs

If we use an individual's hourly wage as the value of an hour of his or her time, the opportunity cost of a good is the price of the good plus the amount of time spent consuming the good times the consumer's hourly wage. If **P** is the price of a good, **t** the time spent consuming it, and **w** the individual's wage rate, then the opportunity cost equals **P + tw.** For example, if a movie ticket costs $7.50 and the movie lasts 2.5 hours, the opportunity cost of the movie to someone who makes $10 per hour is $32.50 ($7.50 + 2.5 hours X $10 per hour), while the opportunity cost of the same movie to someone who makes $20 per hour is $57.50 ($7.50 + 2.5 hours X $20 per hour).

Table 11.1 shows the opportunity cost of other information goods and services and assumes that the consumer's wage rate is $20 per hour.

Table 11.1 Economic Cost of Time-Intensive Goods				
	Financial Cost	**Time (Hours)**	**Time Cost (Wage = $20)**	**Opportunity Cost (Time + Financial)**
Movie	$9	2.5	$50	$59
Book	$20	10	$200	$220
Telephone call	$0.25	0.5	$10	$10.25
Web browsing	$0	1	$20	$20
College class	$1,200	100	$2,000	$3,200
Reference question	$0	0.5	$10	$10

As the wage or the time required to consume the good increases, the opportunity cost increases. A three-hour movie has a greater opportunity cost than a two-hour movie. A 30-minute telephone call has a greater opportunity cost than a 10-minute telephone call. In both cases, if consumers watch the longer movie or make the longer telephone call, it is because they receive more benefit from these goods, even though they have a greater opportunity cost.

Because the opportunity cost of a good depends on an individual's wage, it is individual-specific. Someone with a higher wage has a higher cost of time. As a result, higher wage earners are more likely to hire others to mow their lawns, watch their children, or paint their houses. In all of these examples the high wage earner is willing to pay someone else to do a time-intensive activity instead of doing it himself, to reduce the full economic cost of it.

Value of Time Saved

Many information services save time. The value of the time saved is the benefit consumers receive from these services. For example, can we measure the value of good service to a library patron? Assume the library can employ one of two reference librarians. Assume both librarians are capable of finding the correct answers to patron questions, but one takes an average of five minutes to answer a question while the other takes an average of ten minutes. The more efficient librarian may be more experienced than the less efficient librarian and may expect a higher salary commensurate with the additional years of experience.

The value of the first librarian to a patron is the five minutes of time saved times the hourly wage of the patron. If the patron makes $20 per hour, then the more efficient reference librarian saves the patron $1.67 (five minutes times $0.33 per minute) for each question answered. Conversely, the less efficient librarian has an added cost of $1.67 per patron. If these librarians answer an average of 30 reference questions per day over 250 working days a year, the "better" reference librarian saves patrons $12,500 (30 X 250 X 5 X $20/60 minutes) in time per year. Therefore, although the library may save money by hiring a less experienced librarian, the opportunity cost to patrons is higher.

Malcolm Getz provides an excellent application of the opportunity cost of time in library services.[1] Getz measured the value of time saved by library patrons using an electronic library catalog versus a card catalog. Study participants were asked to search for a book in the library's collection using the electronic catalog and the library's card catalog. Getz found that patrons using the electronic catalog could locate library books, on average, 78.5 seconds faster than they could using the card catalog. Given the number of searches per year and the average wage of library patrons, he estimated that the electronic card catalog saved patrons $115,340 worth of time per year.

The value of an hour spent on a good or service is not always equal to the wage an individual earns. The opportunity cost of an hour can be approximated by individuals' wages only when they cannot spend their time in more than one activity. However, sometimes consumers or patrons can be using time for more than one activity. For example, time spent on a bus can be used to read a newspaper, time spent listening to the radio can also be used to fix your car or clean your house, and time spent waiting for a letter or fax can be used to do other activities. In each example, the value of time used in consuming one good cannot be accurately measured by the individual's wage because he or she might be doing more than one thing.

For example, consider the patron's cost of using interlibrary loan. If there is no financial cost to the patron for requesting a journal article from interlibrary loan—as is the case at most academic libraries—the opportunity cost is the value of the time spent waiting for the article to be delivered. It may take three days for the article to be delivered to the patron; however, we cannot consider the opportunity cost of these three days as the hourly wage multiplied by the hours spent waiting. During this time the patron can be studying, doing research, or reading other articles.

There are two ways to measure the value of time spent waiting. First, the consumer or patron can be interviewed about the cost of time spent waiting for an article to be delivered, or waiting on the bus, or waiting to receive a letter. Kingma and Irving show that patrons are willing to pay an average of $2.55 per article to have immediate delivery of articles.[2] Since the average waiting period for article delivery was 10 days, we can infer that the opportunity cost to patrons of waiting 10 days for delivery is $2.55.

An alternative is to collect data on the use of or demand for nearly identical goods or services that have different prices and different time costs. The train and bus are both popular with commuters, but they have different fares and take different amounts of time to get commuters to their offices. Letters sent first class and overnight delivery have different prices and take different amounts of time to deliver. If time is important, individuals may be willing to pay for the extra charge of overnight delivery. These individuals weigh the value of their time spent waiting against their demand curve for overnight delivery.

To further illustrate, assume patrons of interlibrary loan have two alternative methods of document delivery: service A and service B. Service A may involve requesting a journal article from a library that takes eight days, on average, to deliver the article, but the patron is not charged for it. Assume service B, a commercial delivery service, provides a journal article in two days, on average, but charges the patron $11 for delivery. If the patron is given a choice and requests the article from the commercial delivery service, the patron is revealing that the value of the extra six days waiting for the article to be delivered is at least $11.

This type of information can be used by interlibrary loan librarians to determine the benefit of faster delivery to interlibrary loan patrons. Although the financial cost, to the patron and the library, may be greater with one type of service, the benefit of the time saved by the patron may exceed this extra financial cost. If the value of the time saved exceeds the extra financial cost, then it is economically efficient to use the faster service. Unfortunately, because patrons are not charged for interlibrary loan services at most academic libraries, the extra benefit provided to patrons from faster service does not result in additional revenues for the library to cover the added costs.

Consumer Surplus and Economic Cost

In each of the previous examples—reference librarians, computer speeds, or interlibrary loan services—the difference in the opportunity cost measures the value of the time saved by consumers or patrons. However, this difference underestimates the full value to consumers of a decrease in the economic price of a good or service. If the opportunity cost decreases, the quantity consumers demand will increase. Consumers receive benefit from the decrease in the price of their original level of consumption plus benefit from the increase in the quantity consumed. The full value to consumers of a decrease in price is the increase in consumer surplus. This is illustrated in Figure 11.1.

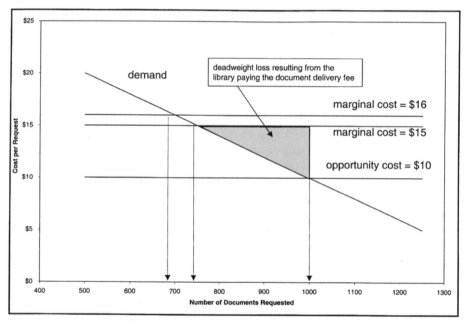

Figure 11.1. Cost of Document Delivery.

Figure 11.1 shows the demand or marginal benefit from document delivery or interlibrary loan services for library patrons. In Figure 11.1 assume that a journal article "costs" the average library patron eight days of waiting at a value of $2 per day, for a price of $16. Now assume that using a commercial document delivery service takes only five days, on average, for delivery, but the commercial service charges $5 for each article delivered. If we assume that patrons pay the $5 document delivery charge, they will see a net decrease in the economic cost of delivery from $16 to $15 (the $5 charge plus five days at $2 per day). Since patrons pay the commercial delivery fee, there is no difference between the opportunity cost of time spent waiting for delivery and the financial cost of the service. The two costs are summed to determine the economic cost of delivery. This consumer surplus gain includes the $1.00 decrease in marginal cost on the original number of articles requested plus the consumer surplus of the increase in requests.

If the library were to pay the $5 fee, instead of the patron, the patron's cost of delivery would decrease to $10. A price decrease from $15 to $10 results in an increase in patron consumer surplus. Unfortunately, if the patron does not pay the document delivery charge, then patrons who receive a benefit from an article that is less than the full economic cost of $15 will request articles. The financial cost to the library of the $5 commercial document delivery fee is $5 per article times the number of articles requested. Because the consumer surplus gain to patrons is less than the financial cost of commercial delivery to the library, there is a deadweight loss.

One of the major advantageous of the Internet is that it lowers the opportunity cost of information delivery by providing more rapid access to information. Journal articles that at one time were only accessible through a library subscription or interlibrary loan are now available over the Internet. As a result, patrons have the ability to dramatically decrease the time spent waiting for article delivery. In addition, because electronic delivery of articles involves little or no marginal cost of delivery, there is no deadweight loss resulting from the library paying for document delivery services.

Congestion

Time saved by one person is sometimes saved by others. Time wasted by one person is sometimes lost by others. Time spent can have positive or negative externalities on other consumers. For example, whenever a new motorist enters a crowded highway he not only increases his own commuting time but slows down all other drivers by increasing congestion. Unfortunately, the new driver never considers the external cost of congestion he imposes on others. The external costs of congestion can be the result of a slow searcher using the compact disks at the library, an employee using the office printer while others are waiting, or a patron who fails to return a book to the library when other patrons want it. As the number of electronic packets sent on the Internet increases, the congestion slows response time for all users.

Information goods and services are sometimes subject to congestion because, as public goods, they are frequently shared by several users or patrons. The Internet, a computer network, a book in the library, a computer workstation, and the library reference desk can all become congested when too many users or patrons try to consume the same service. With a limited number of consumers the service may be non-rival; however, as the number of consumers exceeds capacity, the service becomes congested. This congestion imposes a negative externality on users or patrons who must wait to use a computer terminal or the Internet, read the library book, or ask a question. The external cost of the congestion for public user room computer terminals in an academic library is illustrated in Figure 11.2.

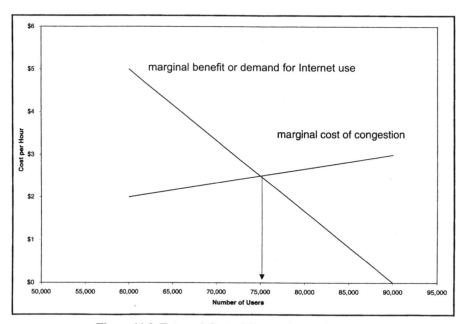

Figure 11.2. External Cost of Congestion on Internet.

Figure 11.2 illustrates the marginal benefit and external cost of using the Internet during one typical hour. The marginal benefit curve is the benefit to individual users minus the opportunity cost of time spent using the Internet. This marginal benefit curve represents the private benefit to individuals of their use. With fewer than 60,000 users, the Internet is a non-rival good and the marginal cost of any individual using it is zero. However, when there are more than 60,000 users, there is an external cost of congestion as traffic increases and access to the Internet slows.

To calculate the cost of congestion, assume that after 60,000 users, each additional user slows down the flow of traffic by, on average, 0.01 seconds each hour. Although this delay is minor for any individual user, in total, 600 seconds or 10 minutes are lost to the slowdown. If the average wage of a typical Internet user is $12 per hour, then the external cost of an additional user is $2.00. Initially this cost is minor, but as the number of users increases, congestion increases.

Additional users of the Internet do not perceive the cost they impose on other users. Each user only perceives the marginal benefit of his or her individual use and will access the Internet as long as the marginal benefit is greater than zero. In Figure 11.2, additional users will continue to access the Internet until there are a total of 90,000 users. At that point, each additional user imposes an external marginal cost equal to $3.00 (0.01 X 90,000 X $1/300 per second). At 90,000 users, the information request of each user is slowed down by five minutes each hour—30,000 extra users times 0.01 seconds slowdown per extra user—thereby requiring the 90,000 users to "spend" an extra five minutes each to acquire information that, during an uncongested period, would take an hour.

The socially efficient level of Internet use in Figure 11.2 is 75,000 users, where the marginal cost of an additional user equals the marginal benefit that user receives from the Internet. The marginal external cost imposed by the 75,000th user is $2.50, as is the marginal benefit that additional user receives from one hour of access. Although the 75,000th user imposes a cost on others, she also receives a benefit greater than this cost and therefore should be allowed to access the Internet. Additional users will impose costs of congestion greater than the marginal benefit they would receive from access.

To achieve the socially efficient level of use, only 75,000 users should be allowed on the Internet in a given hour. The easiest way to ensure this level of use is to charge users a fee of $2.50 for one hour of access. In this case, only users with a marginal benefit of access greater than or equal to $2.50 will be willing to pay the access fee. Users between 75,000 and 90,000 receive less than $2.50 in benefit from access. These users are not willing to pay the external costs that their access would impose on other users.

Services frequently suffer from congestion. The library reference desk, the video store checkout counter, or the computer terminals in a university public user room may have lines of patrons or customers waiting for their turn to use them. This is also a form of congestion and can be inefficient, depending on the number of reference librarians, video clerks, or computer terminals available. Each service port has a cost of providing access. This cost is the librarian's or video clerk's wage or the cost of the computer terminals. As the number of librarians, clerks, or terminals increases, the external cost of congestion decreases.

In Figure 11.3, the marginal cost of a reference librarian is $15 per hour. If the demand for reference librarians was compared to the marginal cost, then two librarians would be working the desk in any given hour. However, if there is a waiting line at the reference desk, an increase in the number of reference librarians will decrease the wait and decrease the cost to patrons of having a question answered. This decrease, or positive externality from decreasing congestion, is subtracted from the marginal cost of the service. As a result, the efficient number of reference librarians is three. Each librarian not only provides a service to patrons but also reduces the opportunity cost to patrons of waiting in line.

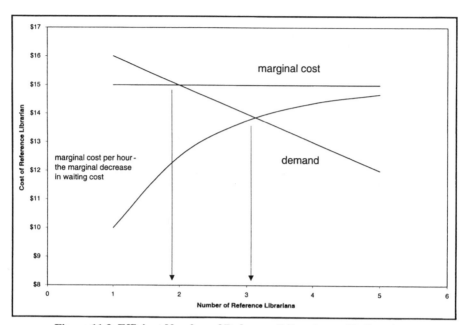

Figure 11.3. Efficient Number of Reference Librarians with Queuing.

Present Value

The value of goods also depends on the timing of future costs and benefits. When you purchase a durable good you expect to receive a benefit from the good over a period of several years. The demand for a durable good or service reflects the total of all future benefits. For example, when you purchase a video, your willingness to pay for it is not the value of a single viewing. Rather, your benefit from that video is the sum of the value you expect to receive from all future viewings. This is because the video is a durable good used over a period of time, unlike a nondurable or perishable good that has a limited time of use and therefore provides only a single, immediate benefit to the consumer. Books, videos, computer hardware and software, journal subscriptions, and many other information goods and services are durable goods. In each case, the cumulative value of all future uses of a good determines the demand for that good.

Benefits and costs should be measured over time. For example, when a photocopy machine is purchased, there are annual benefits that you expect to receive from using the machine, and annual costs of maintenance, supplies, and depreciation. To determine whether it is worthwhile to purchase a photocopy machine, the lifetime stream of future costs and the purchase price should be compared to the stream of future benefits.

However, future costs and benefits are not equal to present costs and benefits. They are not worth as much. To illustrate this, assume that you can buy and receive a computer for $1,000 and have a choice of paying the $1,000 today versus paying $1,000 one year from now with no interest. If given a choice, most people would choose to pay the $1,000 a year from now. This is because if you found a bank that paid 5 percent on a risk-free savings account, you could place $952.38 in the bank today and receive $1,000 [$1,000 = $952.38(1 + 0.05)] one year from now. The value today of $1,000 a year from now at an interest rate of 5 percent is $952.38 [$952.38 = $1,000/(1 + 0.05)]. More generally, if r is the interest rate, C dollars one year from now is worth $C/(1 = r)$ dollars today. Likewise, C dollars two years from now is worth $C/[(1 + r)(1 + r)] = C/(1 + r)^2$ today because this is the amount of money you would have to put in a risk-free savings account to have C dollars in two years.

We define the *present value* of C dollars, t years from now at an interest rate of r, as $C/(1 + r)^t$. The present value of a stream of dollars $C_0, C_1, C_2, \ldots, C_n$, where subscripts refer to the year in which the dollars are received, is shown in equation 11.1.

$$PV = C_0 + C_1/(1 + r) + C_2/(1 + r)^2 \ldots + C_n/(1 + r)^n \qquad (11.1)$$

If a good or service has a stream of annual costs of $(C_0, C_1, C_2, \ldots, C_n)$ and a stream of annual benefits of $(B_0, B_1, B_2, \ldots, B_n)$, then the *net present value* of it is as shown in equation 11.2.

$$NPV = (B_0 - C_0) + (B_1 - C_1)/(1 + r) + (B_2 - C_2)/(1 + r)^2 \ldots + (B_n - C_n)/(1 + r)^n \qquad (11.2)$$

Table 11.2 illustrates the net present value for the purchase of a video based on different interest rates, r, assuming that you use the tape twice in the first year, twice in the second year, once in the third year, but not thereafter. Table 11.2 also assumes that the value of the first use is $10, since the video is new, and the value of each subsequent use is $3.

Table 11.2
Net Present Value of Videotape Purchase

Year	Uses	Benefit	Cost	$r = 0\%$	$r = 5\%$	$r = 10\%$
0	2	$13	($20)	($7.00)	($7.00)	($7.00)
1	2	$ 6	$ 0	$6.00	$5.71	$5.45
2	1	$ 3	$ 0	$3.00	$2.72	$2.48
3	0	$ 0	$ 0	$0.00	$0.00	$0.00
Total	5			$2.00	$1.43	$0.93

Note: Parentheses indicate negative numbers.

When the interest rate equals 0, the net present value equals the sum of all costs and benefits. However, as the interest rate increases, the value of future benefits decreases while present costs are unchanged, causing the net present value to decrease.

Individual demand for durable goods is based on the net present value a consumer expects to receive from the good. The demand for durable information goods and services by organizations requires managers to determine the present value of benefits and costs for all potential users or patrons. For example, consider the purchase of a photocopy machine by the university library. The net present value is illustrated in Table 11.3.

Table 11.3
Net Present Value of Photocopier

Year	Use	Revenue	Consumer Surplus	Cost	Net Financial Benefit	Net Economic Benefit	Net Present Financial Benefit	Net Present Economic Benefit
0	100,000	$10,000	$6,000	$25,000	($15,000)	($9,000)	($15,000)	($9,000)
1	100,000	$10,000	$6,000	$10,000	$0	$6,000	$0	$5,714
2	100,000	$10,000	$6,000	$10,000	$0	$6,000	$0	$5,442
3	100,000	$10,000	$6,000	$10,000	$0	$6,000	$0	$5,183
						Total	($15,000)	$7,339

Note: Parentheses indicate negative numbers.

Table 11.3 assumes that the library is considering purchasing a photocopier that will last four years at an interest rate of 5 percent. Future benefits and costs are discounted by the discount factor in column 8. The level of use shown in column 2 and consumer surplus in column 4 can be estimated from data on existing photocopy demand at the library. Table 11.3 assumes that the cost of the photocopier is $15,000 and has an additional $10,000 in annual marginal costs based on an estimated 100,000 uses per year.

If photocopying is priced at the marginal cost of a copy, $0.10, then annual revenue of $10,000 will equal the marginal cost of the photocopier but will not cover the fixed cost of purchasing it. Column 8 in Table 11.3 shows that the net present financial value of the photocopier is negative $15,000.

However, the economic benefit of photocopying includes the consumer surplus that users receive from it. As shown in Table 11.3, the annual consumer surplus from photocopying is $6,000. The net economic benefit is shown in column 7. This economic benefit is the sum of the revenue and the consumer surplus that users receive from photocopying minus the cost of the copier. If price is set equal to the marginal cost of a copy, it is economically efficient to purchase the photocopier as long as the consumer surplus exceeds the initial $15,000 cost of the machine. Given the discount factor, the net present economic value of the photocopier is shown in column 9: $7,339.

An alternative to calculating net present value is to amortize the fixed cost of purchase over the lifetime of the use and compare annual costs to benefits. Amortization is the same as assuming the library borrows the $15,000 to purchase the photocopier and pays off the loan over the four-year life of the copier. Each year for **n** years a payment **P** must be made to pay off the loan amount **X** at an interest rate **r.** The formula for amortization is shown in equation 11.3.

$$P = \frac{X(1 + r)^n}{(1 - (1 + r)^n)/(-r)} \tag{11.3}$$

In this example, each of four annual payments equals $4,230. The annual cost equals $14,230 and the annual economic surplus equals $1,770 ($16,000 - $14,230). Amortization shows that annual benefits exceed annual costs. The amortization of fixed costs enables the analyst to show yearly costs of services. This is typically done when the analyst is determining the annual cost of operation, including the costs of the building and land. When doing this type of analysis, it is also important to include annual costs of maintenance of the fixed asset. Choosing the number of years for the asset as well as the interest rate will make important differences in the analysis.

Although consumer surplus provides benefits to patrons, it does not provide revenue to the library. This means that in this example the library must find alternative sources of revenue (university support, tax support, tuition). The alternative is to increase the price of photocopying to raise the revenue for the purchase of the machine. Although this may be necessary to finance the copier, it will produce deadweight loss for this service. Ramsey pricing of photocopying and other services will bring the library as close to its efficient level of service as possible.

Summary

The value of time spent consuming goods and services, waiting for goods or services to be delivered, or waiting for future benefits and costs is an important factor in cost-benefit analysis. Many information goods and services require time to consume and, as a result, require that the opportunity cost to patrons or users be considered in calculating demand for them. Faster service in delivering information goods may not always result in revenue for the library, government agency, or organization; however, it provides a measurable benefit to patrons, users, and consumers.

The opportunity cost of information goods and services can be measured by survey or by demand analysis of information goods. Demands for express delivery, faster computer processors, and faster modems for accessing online information are attempts by consumers to reduce the opportunity cost of time.

Future costs and benefits must be discounted to determine their present value. Benefits that consumers must wait for are not worth as much today and therefore must be discounted. The present value of any purchase of a durable good is the discounted value of the stream of future benefits and costs to the consumer. Doing this analysis on an annual basis requires amortizing the costs of fixed assets.

Notes

1. Malcolm Getz, "Some Benefits of the Online Catalog," *College & Research Libraries* (May 1987): 224-40; Malcolm Getz, "More Benefits of Automation," *College & Research Libraries* (1988): 534-44.

2. Bruce R. Kingma, and Suzanne Irving, *The Economics of Access versus Ownership to Scholarly Information* (Binghamton, NY: Haworth Press, 1996).

Chapter 12

Resource Sharing

Books, journals, newspapers, compact disks, videotapes, and movies are information resources that can be shared. In each case, buyers can share their purchases with others or agree to jointly purchase a good. When you purchase a book you intend to share with a friend, you are resource sharing. When an academic library participates in interlibrary loan, it is resource sharing. In fact, any library, whether public or private, academic or corporate, is an organization sharing information resources, whose cooperative agreements can produce more efficient purchase and consumption policies. In each case, these information resources can be modeled as public goods.

Unfortunately, not all organizations or consumers who engage in resource sharing do so efficiently. Libraries in consortia do not always use cooperative collection development strategies. Instead, resource sharing is seen as a way to increase access to materials the library does not own, rather than a way to cooperatively lower costs by decreasing duplicate materials. Whether the materials shared are journal subscriptions, compact disks, or personal computers, understanding the economic benefits and costs of sharing information resources is important for managers and policymakers.

Multiple Users of Information Resources

Resource sharing is defined as using information goods or services as public goods, which are shared among users. Each consumer or user receives a benefit from the individual good that is shared collectively. The collective benefit to all users is the public good benefit or demand for that good. Efficient resource sharing implies using the collective benefit as a measure of social benefit and comparing this to the marginal cost of production and delivery.

Journal subscriptions, books, and the interlibrary loan of these resources at academic libraries are excellent examples of resource sharing. Each library purchases journal subscriptions and books to satisfy the collective needs of its patrons. Use studies, citation analysis, and faculty and student requests are used to determine the potential value of different journals and books so that the library can make efficient decisions about purchasing them.

If patrons ask for books or journals their library does not own, typically the library will find another library that owns this journal title or book and request to borrow it. In this way the purchases of one library are shared with other libraries. However, when one library purchases a book or journal title, it only considers the benefits to its patrons and not the possible benefits to patrons of other libraries. A broader definition of economic efficiency would require that the benefit to all patrons be considered. An economic analysis of consortia considers the benefits provided to all library patrons within the consortium, not only the benefit to patrons of any individual library. In other words, economic efficiency for the consortium, which considers the needs of all patrons, may differ from efficient acquisitions and interlibrary loan policy for an individual library within the consortium.

To show this, we first examine the economics of an individual library's decision to purchase a journal or book. Figure 12.1 illustrates the economics of a library's decision to subscribe to a journal. It shows the demand for use of a particular year's subscription for this particular journal, as well as the marginal cost of access to this journal via document delivery. Although use, represented on the horizontal axis, should be the present value of use, for simplicity we assume that future uses and present uses are of equal value. Assume that patrons are equally satisfied with articles that they have acquired by using the library's subscription to a journal and articles received from interlibrary loan via document delivery. Also assume that there is no difference in the opportunity cost of patron access using a library subscription or using document delivery.

If the library subscribes to this journal, the benefit of a subscription is the benefit patrons receive from the subscription. Because patrons have a price of 0 to access the journal when the library owns the subscription, their level of use is 25. According to Figure 12.1, the highest value of a patron's use is $100. The benefit patrons receive from this subscription is equal to the area under the use demand curve. This equals $1,250 (0.5 X $100 X 25). The cost of the subscription is the fixed cost of subscribing to the journal. If we assume that the journal subscription costs $300 plus $100 for the cost of cataloguing, binding, and storing the journal, the net benefit to the library community of this journal is $1,250 - $400 = $850.

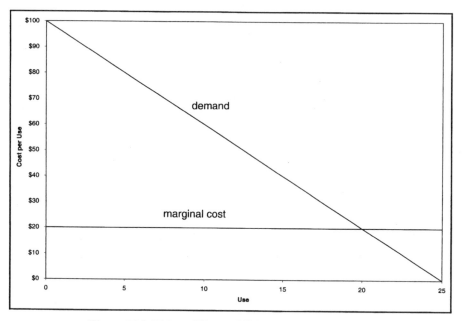

Figure 12.1. Value of Journal Subscription to Library.

Most academic libraries provide free interlibrary loan services to patrons. Patrons can receive a copy of most articles from academic journals without charge. However, even though patrons are not charged for these services, there are real costs to the library of delivering articles. Figure 12.1 assumes these costs are $20 per article. If the figure represents the use or demand for articles from this journal—assuming there is no change in use whether access is provided by interlibrary loan or a journal subscription—then the benefit from "free" interlibrary loan is the same as the patrons' benefit from having the journal subscription: $1,250. Given the cost of interlibrary loan to the library of $500 ($20 per article x 25 articles) the net benefit of access via interlibrary loan is $750 ($1,250 - 500). The difference between the net benefit from a library subscription and providing access by interlibrary loan is $100 ($850 - $750).

More generally, if **U** equals the level of use, **w** equals the marginal cost of use, **S** is the fixed cost of a subscription, and **B** is the patron benefit, the difference between the value of a journal subscription and the value of providing access by interlibrary loan is as shown in equation 12.1.

$$(B - S) - (B - wU) = wU - S \tag{12.1}$$

Equation 12.1 shows that the difference between the net benefit of a journal subscription and interlibrary loan is simply the difference in their costs. This assumes that there is no difference in the level of use between interlibrary loan and a journal subscription. In this case, we do not need to measure the benefits to patrons of access to determine which method is more economically efficient; we only need to measure the costs of delivery. The method of delivery that is the least costly for libraries is the most economically efficient.

In this example, economic efficiency results from the method of access that is more cost-efficient. The cost efficiency of a journal subscription relative to document delivery of journal articles depends on the costs of each method of access and the expected level of use of the particular journal title. If there is sufficient use for a journal, it will be more cost-efficient to provide access by purchasing a subscription. The importance of use in this equation is illustrated in Figure 12.2.

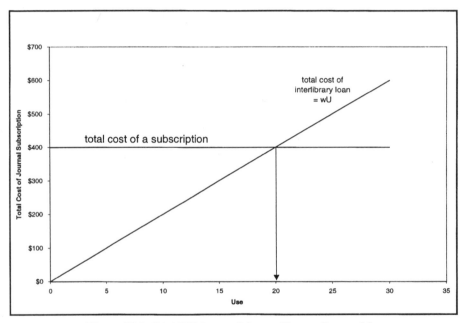

Figure 12.2. Cost Efficiency of Access Versus Ownership.

Figure 12.2 shows the total cost of both methods of access. The cost of a journal subscription, $400, is the subscription price plus any other costs associated with the subscription. The total cost of document delivery, $\mathbf{wU}$, equals the marginal cost, $\mathbf{w} = \$20$, per document or article delivered times the number of requests, $\mathbf{U}$. The break-even level of requests is 20. If use is below 20, access is more efficiently provided via interlibrary loan. If use is greater than 20, access is more efficiently provided via a journal subscription.

Although libraries do not always consider the economic efficiency of interlibrary loan and journal subscription policy, economics certainly influences their use of interlibrary loan. As journal prices increase or the cost of interlibrary loan decreases, interlibrary loan offers greater financial savings to the library. The influence of an increase in journal subscription prices is illustrated in Figure 12.3, in which the price of a journal subscription increases the fixed costs from $400 to

$500. As a result, the break-even level of use increases from 20 to 25. As journal subscription prices increase, there is a larger range of use in which it is more cost-efficient to offer access via interlibrary loan.

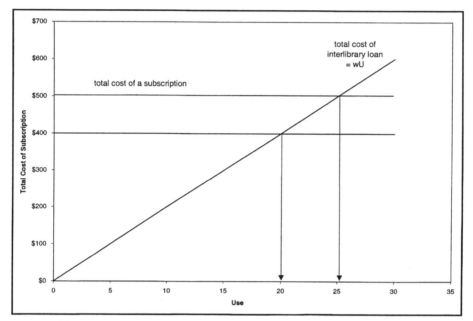

Figure 12.3. Effect of Increase in Journal Prices on Break-Even Point.

Interlibrary loan is, by definition, a consortium arrangement among participating libraries. Library networks and even commercial document delivery services provide low-cost access to journals for patrons who otherwise would be denied access to them.

Many libraries also form smaller consortia of local libraries or libraries with complementary journal collections. These consortia are economically efficient only if they deliver lower cost or higher quality access to journal articles than is available through existing interlibrary loan networks. If this occurs, then collection development among partners in the consortium can result in an increase in economic efficiency. If joint collection development is used, individual libraries in the consortium that might not subscribe to a particular journal title may subscribe once the benefits to the consortium are recognized. Joint collection development essentially treats the collection of the consortium as a single large collection. The cost factors involved in the decision for the consortium to subscribe to a particular journal title are illustrated in Figure 12.4.

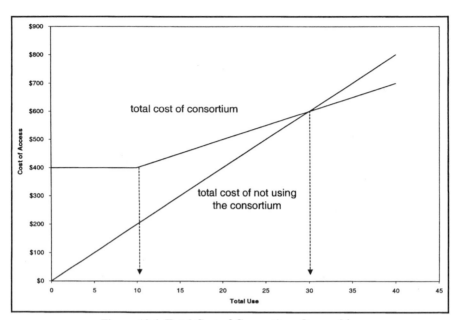

Figure 12.4. Total Cost of Consortium Ownership.

Figure 12.4 represents the costs of access to a particular journal title via consortium and nonconsortium document delivery. The horizontal axis is the total use of this journal title by all member libraries. The total cost of access via nonconsortium document delivery is the marginal cost of delivery times the total number of requests by all member libraries. Assume that the marginal cost of delivery from nonconsortium sources is $20 per article. The total cost of access via the consortium is the cost of the journal subscription to the consortium plus the cost of article delivery to other members of the consortium. Assume that the journal subscription costs $400 and the cost of delivery within the consortium is $10 per article. The cost of article delivery to the other members of the consortium is the marginal cost of delivery within the consortium times the level of use by all members who do not own the journal subscription.

Figure 12.4 assumes that no single library within the consortium is already subscribing to this particular journal. If any one library is subscribing, then the choice of using lower cost consortium delivery rather than nonconsortium delivery is obvious. What is illustrated in Figure 12.4 is the financial advantage to the consortium of subscribing to a particular journal title that no individual library would subscribe to otherwise. In this case, the break-even point is 30 total uses. At 30 uses, whether article delivery is provided through the consortium or not, the total cost is $500. If the sum of use by all member libraries exceeds 30, it is economically efficient for the consortium to subscribe to this journal. If total use is less than 30, it is more efficient to use higher cost nonconsortium delivery simply because the low level of use cannot justify the consortium paying for even a single subscription.

Although it is easy to illustrate the financial savings of a library consortium, it is more difficult to operate a consortium efficiently and provide appropriate incentives for efficient collective decisions. For example, the one library that will subscribe to the journal in Figure 12.4 has no financial incentive to do so even if total consortium use exceeds 30. This is because the single library would not subscribe to the journal outside of the consortium. As a result, individual libraries must make decisions that serve the consortium's best interests but not their own best interests. Even though it is more cost-efficient for the consortium to behave as a single large library, unless library budgets are controlled by a single consortium manager, individual library managers will be concerned with their library's budget and not with the resource needs of other members of the consortium. Potential solutions to the consortium financing and collection development problems require that libraries compensate lending libraries with the financing necessary to maintain borrowed materials.

The Research Libraries Network (RLN) has attempted to answer the consortium financing problem by compensating libraries that are excessive lenders of materials over RLN. If your library lends more than it borrows, you receive a refund based on net lending. This rewards individual libraries that may have collections valued by the rest of the members of RLN.

Opportunity Cost of Patron Time

When resources are shared among libraries, agencies, or individuals, there is usually a waiting period for the borrower. For example, when a library uses interlibrary loan to provide patrons with access to journal articles, the patron must wait a few days or weeks to get the requested article. The cost of the time spent waiting must be included in the economic cost of interlibrary loan.

Figure 12.5 shows the full economic costs and benefits of providing journal access to patrons via interlibrary loan versus maintaining a journal subscription. In Figure 12.5, the opportunity cost of time spent by the patron waiting for an article to be delivered by interlibrary loan is $10; the marginal cost of document delivery, including staff time, supplies, and any document delivery charges is $20. Figure 12.5 assumes that the opportunity cost of retrieving an article from a journal the library subscribes to is 0.

If the library owns the subscription, the level of use is 25 and the consumer surplus from this use is equal to $1,250 [($100) X (25) X (0.5)]. The net benefit is $1,250 minus the fixed cost of the subscription. If the library does not own the subscription and patrons are not charged for interlibrary loan, the level of requests for articles is 22.5, where the marginal cost of a patron's time, $10, just equals the marginal benefit to the patron of receiving the article. In this case, the consumer surplus decreases to $1,012.50 [($100 - $10) X (22.5) X (0.5)]. The net benefit from using interlibrary loan is the consumer surplus minus the costs of interlibrary loan, $1,012.50 - ($10) X (22.5) = $787.50. The difference in net benefit between providing access via a journal subscription and via interlibrary loan is $1,250 - $787.50 = $462.50.

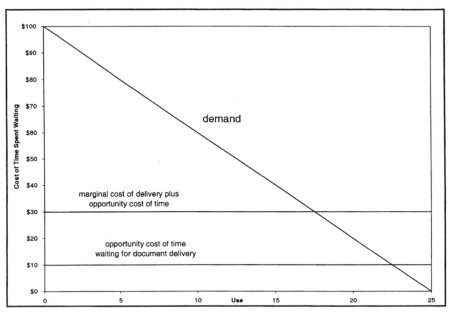

Figure 12.5. Opportunity Cost of Information Access.

As in equation 12.1, let **B** equal the benefit from providing access by interlibrary loan, **w** the library's marginal cost of this access, **U** the level of use, and **S** the fixed costs of a subscription. Let **c** equal the opportunity cost of access to patrons and **B'** equal the benefit from the library's subscription to a journal. The difference in net benefit between providing access through a journal subscription and interlibrary loan is shown in equation 12.2.

$$(B' - S) - [B - (w + c)U] = (B' - B) - [S - (w + c)U] \qquad (12.2)$$

The right-hand side of equation 12.2 is the difference in consumer surplus minus the difference in costs. The cost of interlibrary loan must include the opportunity cost to patrons of waiting for delivery. In this example, the cost of waiting adds $10 to the cost of interlibrary loan. Even if the financial cost to a library may be less with interlibrary loan, the opportunity cost to patrons of waiting for delivery may make it economically efficient to purchase a subscription instead of using document delivery.

Although it is possible to illustrate the net benefit of access versus ownership of journal articles, it is more difficult to actually estimate this difference. A library may know the number of articles requested through interlibrary loan from a particular journal, but this does not indicate the level of use the journal would receive if the library subscribed to it. Likewise, a library may have statistics on the number of patrons who benefit from a journal subscription, but this does not indicate the number of articles that would be requested using interlibrary loan if the library did not subscribe to the journal.

Summary

The economic efficiency of resource sharing depends on the level of use of shared resources, their cost, and the opportunity cost of patrons waiting for delivery of the shared resource. Resource sharing can provide economically efficient access for library consortia; however, the difficulties of providing incentives to share and purchase shared resources must be overcome. In addition, although resource sharing can be cost-efficient for libraries, the opportunity cost to patrons of waiting for shared resources must be considered to determine if it is economically efficient for patrons.

Resource sharing for academic libraries has increased as a result of the increases in journal prices. I have described the potential savings for library consortia that share journal subscriptions, but there may also be an effect on the market for journal subscriptions and prices that I have not explored. As libraries continue to share their resources, the result may be that journal prices rise to offset the decline in subscriptions. However, the aggregate effect of journal cancellations is less important to individual libraries than the potential savings from sharing individual journal titles.

Chapter 13

The Costs and Benefits of
Digital Information

The history of communications from clay tablets to scrolls to printing has been about the economic evolution of producing, storing, and accessing information. At each step in the evolution of information, benefits to consumers increase while producer costs decrease. Digital information or the digitization of information is the next step in this evolution. Digital information has increased benefits over print and provides information consumers with these benefits at a lower cost.

The benefits of digital information include the ability to search more effectively than print. Keyword searching on CD is more efficient than the previous subject indexes in card catalogs or other print indexes. Rapid results to digital searching enable the user to make more searches using more keywords with a lower opportunity cost of time.

Digital information also has a lower opportunity cost of access than print. Large stores of print information require a user to travel to the library to find the print source. Digital information can be accessed from a networked workstation more rapidly, eliminating the user's opportunity cost of traveling to the print resource.

The benefits of digital information are easy to identify, but they are difficult to measure. No studies have been conducted to measure the decrease in the opportunity cost or increase in consumer surplus for users of digital information, even though the economic benefits of digital access are significant. Studies have analyzed the cost of digital information and have shown that digital access can be provided at lower cost.

Cost of Access to Information

A complete analysis of the cost of digital information requires identifying the stakeholders in the information delivery chain and the fixed and variable costs for each method of access. In the information chain there are three stakeholders: producers, intermediaries, and consumers. There are at least three possible methods of access: print, microtext, and digital access.

Producers in the information delivery chain can include publishers but also can include government agencies, corporations, libraries, or any organization that is producing information. Even consumers can be information producers. For example, scholars who produce working papers can reproduce them in print or digital format for distribution. Intermediaries are organizations that purchase or receive the information and provide access to information consumers. This is the typical role of a library.

For each method of access and each stakeholder, there are fixed and variable costs. Consumers can access information in print format by traveling to a bookstore or library and acquiring the book. Each use of print information requires a new purchase or selection of a library book. The fixed costs of print include the opportunity costs of traveling to a bookstore or library. To the customer or patron, the marginal costs of print include purchasing or selecting another book. If a patron accesses information by using a library's microtext collection, the fixed costs of traveling to the library are identical to the fixed cost of access to the print. However, the marginal costs of choosing and reading each item may be more or less than the marginal costs of reading books. Patrons who are unfamiliar with microfiche may find it difficult to use and have a higher marginal cost of access. Patrons who are frequent users of microfiche may prefer the compact storage of a larger number of items within a few cabinets.

Consumer Costs

The costs of digital access for patrons depend on their access to a workstation to view a digital copy. If the patron is using the library for digital access, the fixed cost of access is the opportunity cost of travel to the library, the same fixed cost for accessing print or microtext. However, if the patron is using a workstation at home or in an office, the fixed cost of access can be significant, requiring the purchase of a personal computer and network connection. Those with these investments obtain access, while those without do not have access to digital information. If we assume that the patron has access to the same information whether in print or digital form, his decision to access the information in either form may be represented in Figure 13.1.

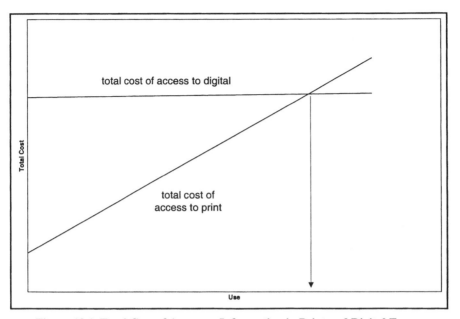

Figure 13.1. Total Cost of Access to Information in Print and Digital Form.

In this example, the patron's fixed cost of access is the purchase of a personal computer and networked connection to the digital resources. If the information is acquired in digital form, the opportunity cost of each use—including the cost of searching, accessing, and storing the information—is less than the cost of use of the print. The fixed cost of using the print—the opportunity cost of acquiring the book—is less than the fixed costs of a personal computer. However, the marginal cost of each use of print is higher based on the higher cost of searching, retrieving, and storing or photocopying the information for future use.

In this example, the patron will use the digital information only if his anticipated level of use is so great that the total cost of digital information is less than the total cost of print. At a lower level of use, the patron will use the print resources.

Patrons with higher levels of use are more likely to make the investment necessary to access information digitally. In fact, these patrons, by investing in the knowledge of how to access and use digital information, will use other digital sources. Given the quantity of information available in digital format using the library and World Wide Web and the low cost of access, digital users are likely to have much higher levels of use of information than those that only use print.

Producer and Intermediary Costs

The costs of producing digital information include producing the information, mounting it in digital form typically on a networked server, electronic storage space, and maintaining and migrating the files in future years. Conway, Kenney, and Kingma have identified the costs of digitization of print information products (see Table 13.1). Kingma also identifies the cost of print and microfiche production.

Table 13.1 Cost of Digitization				
	Number of Images	Cost per Image	Number of Titles	Cost per Title
Conway, P., Yale University, University Project Open Book, 1996 (fiche to digital, 1994/95, marginal cost est.)	432,000	$0.33	2,000	$73
Kenney, A., Cornell University, 1997 (paper to digital to COM, 1994/96, marginal cost estimate)	450,000	$0.28	1,270	$102
Kingma, B., CIHM Early Canadiana Online, 2000 (fiche to digital, 1998/99, average cost estimate)	651,742	$0.60	3,308	$119

Table 13.1 identifies the fixed costs of producing an image or manuscript title in digital format. All three studies estimate the costs of scanning existing print or microtext images into digital form. The studies by Conway and Kenney use marginal cost analysis to determine the amount of time and resources needed to scan each item. The study by Kingma uses average cost analysis, dividing total costs by number of items.

The cost of producing digital information can be compared to the costs of providing access to information in print and microfiche format. To a library, the cost of print is the cost of purchasing the book or journal. If the library or organization were to make microfiche copies of the information, there would be production costs of the microtext. These costs are shown in Table 13.2.

Table 13.2 **Cost of Print, Microfiche, and Digital Information**		
	Production Costs per Title	**Annual Access Costs per Title**
Print	Purchase price	$2.53
Fiche	$143.10	$0.07
Digital	$111.19	$16.84

Table 13.2 shows that for an individual library, digitizing is not a cost-effective way to provide patron access. Producing or purchasing microfiche of print information may be cost-effective, depending on the purchase price of the print. Microtext also provides significant annual savings in storage and access.

Producing digital copies of print materials is less expensive than microfiche. However, the annual costs of maintaining the electronic copies—primarily the costs of technical staff support—are significantly higher than for microfiche or print. In the long run, an increase in the number of technical staff and increase in the use of digital products may decrease the cost per title of digital information. The benefits, identified earlier, of digital information to a library's patrons may also make digitization worth the additional annual costs.

Access to information in different formats has a different level of "publicness" to the good. Print-based information can be accessed by the purchaser or the patron of a library that has purchased it. Microtext can be reproduced, with copies provided to other libraries providing benefit to patrons of more than one library. Digital information can be provided to patrons over a campus intranet or to patrons regardless of location over the Internet. Over a network, the marginal cost of reproduction for digital information is 0, which means that digital information can be copied and reproduced at a lower cost than print or microtext.

As the number of networked libraries increases and the number of digital titles increases, the average cost per library per title will decrease to a level comparable to the cost of microtext. To make these comparisons, consider increasing the number of titles from 3,300 to 46,200 and the number of libraries from 1 to 42. The average cost per library per title is shown in Table 13.3.

At this level of production, average costs per digital title decrease such that the production costs and access costs are similar to or less than print and microfiche.

Table 13.3
Change in Cost of Print, Microtext, and Digital Information Resulting from Increasing Number of Libraries and Titles

	Production Costs per Title	Annual Access Costs per Title
Print	Purchase price	$2.53
Fiche	$4.16	$0.07
Digital	$2.40	$0.07

Pricing of Digital Information

Scholarly information in print format has been priced at different levels for different types of consumers. Scholarly journal publishers charge libraries a higher price for a journal subscription than individual subscribers and give discounts to student subscribers. This price differentiation enables publishers to base price on value and collect sufficient revenues to cover costs and make a profit.

Publishers also use value-based pricing for digital information products. Electronic journals are priced at different levels for libraries, individuals, and students. Site licenses for multiple users at an organization or in a consortium provide additional opportunities for value-based pricing for digital products. A site license contract is based on the number of simultaneous users or number of potential users: the more users, the higher the cost of the license.

However, unlike print information, digital products delivered over networks can service many patrons simultaneously. Books and journals as physical resources can only service one patron at a time. Therefore, digital products can have more value than print.

Consider the example of value-based pricing discussed in Chapter 9. Value-based pricing is used for subscriptions to scholarly academic journals. Libraries and institutions pay a higher subscription rate than the rate charged individual subscribers. Students get a further discount. The three price segments—library, individual, student—are based on the demand or value each group places on access to the journal. Scholars and students subscribe to the journal to save the opportunity cost of traveling to the library to borrow the library's copy. The demand for a subscription to a print journal and the profit-maximizing prices are shown in Figure 13.2.

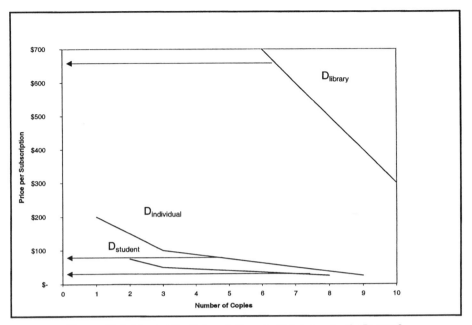

Figure 13.2. Market for Subscriptions to Print Academic Journal.

In a networked digital environment, it is likely that the demand for access to the information will be equal to or greater than the demand for access to print information. The benefits from digital access, including the searchability of the database and the opportunity cost savings of delivery to one's desktop, imply greater demand for digital access.

The networked environment also implies that site licenses for information delivery are more efficient. Instant delivery is possible through a single site license for multiple simultaneous users. There is no need for the publisher or scholar to incur additional transaction costs of billing for individual or student subscriptions. Libraries are willing to purchase site licenses for their patrons to provide greater access to information. With site license access over the network, individuals and students are likely not to purchase subscriptions, decreasing publisher revenues from these markets but increasing the use of the library's license for the information. Each user of the library's site license adds value to the digital license and therefore increases the price the publisher can charge for access.

We can show the increase in demand for the library's license to the electronic journal. Figure 13.3 assumes that the demand **D** for access to the electronic journal is the same for all three groups as it was for the print journal. However, if the library purchases a site license, this increases the value that the scholarly community receives from the library's subscription. If the library accurately measures the value of access to journals, the demand for a subscription to this electronic version of the journal should increase. The publisher is then able to charge a higher price for the electronic subscription. In Figure 13.3 the price charged libraries for the electronic subscription is $680, an increase of $80 over the print subscription charge.

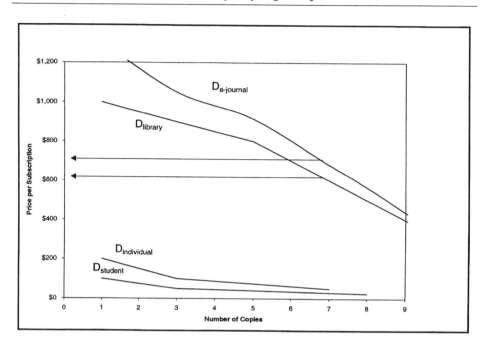

Figure 13.3. Market for Subscriptions to Electronic Academic Journal.

In this example, the same number of library subscriptions is purchased at a higher subscription price. It is possible that additional libraries will subscribe to the journal title because the value to their patrons of having access to the electronic version is great enough to have the library subscribe to an electronic journal that it may not have subscribed to in print.

Factors other than the increase in value to library users influence the price publishers charge for a subscription to an electronic journal. Some users may prefer or insist on having access to the print version of the journal. The publisher can bundle the print and electronic subscription for the library at an additional cost. However, the marginal costs of producing a print copy or electronic copy of the journal are trivial compared to the fixed, first-copy costs of producing an issue. Publishers also bundle several electronic journals to provide a discount on the bundle relative to subscribing to each journal individually. This is also a version of value-based pricing; publishers decrease the price per title, recognizing the increased value to a library of additional journal titles but the decreased willingness-to-pay for each title.

Summary

Digital information has a different cost structure than print information. Consumers of digital information typically have a large fixed cost of purchasing a personal computer or finding access to digital products, but if the information is available on a network, they have significant benefits from and lower costs of access. Production of digital products also has high fixed, first-copy costs, but the costs of distribution and reproduction are significantly lower than for print.

Whether information is available in digital, print, microtext, or other form, value-based pricing is used to provide sufficient revenues to cover production costs and profit. Value-based pricing relies on the producers' ability to segment consumers or determine the value from consumption by an organization. With information in physical form—print or microtext—the producer must be able to identify consumers and set different prices based on the perceived value from that consumer group. With information in digital form available over a network, producers must be able to identify the potential number of users and set prices accordingly.

With value-based pricing and low marginal cost of reproduction, costs have little impact on the price charged. Pricing must be sufficient to cover fixed costs; however, the 0 marginal cost of reproducing digital information in a networked environment implies that price is based on the demand or value a consumer receives from the information. Price is adjusted based on demand, not on costs.

Chapter 14

Network Economics

The economics of digital information in a networked environment imply that higher prices will be charged for information previously available in print. The same information in print and digital format provides greater benefit to users and, therefore, with value-based pricing the information will command a higher price in digital form. The network enables digital information to be reproduced and delivered at a lower cost to more users and, therefore, makes the price of access higher for the same information that in print would serve fewer users.

The delivery of digital information in a networked environment also makes it easier for publishers to estimate the demand or benefit users get from access and makes it easier for publishers to use value-based pricing for access to the information. Information in digital form available over a network provides more detailed information to the supplier of the information about the use and value of access. In addition, the lower opportunity cost of access for information consumers offers greater benefit than the same information in print. Both effects can change the structure of access and pricing in the market to make central financing and distribution more cost-effective than in the print world and make value-based pricing more profitable. In addition, these effects make it more profitable for publishers to acquire journal titles and provide access to a larger selection of titles through a single channel.

Pricing of Electronic Journals

The role of the network is to lower the costs of distribution and reproduction; as a result, the opportunity cost of access for patrons decreases. With print information, the opportunity cost of access makes it more cost-effective for scholars and students to purchase individual subscriptions rather than travel to the library to borrow a print journal. With digital information in a networked environment, the information can be delivered to many users simultaneously without the cost of travel. If individual subscriptions are purchased, these involve networked access to the information from the publisher's server or web site. The remaining cost to users is the transaction cost or cost to purchase access to information from the publisher.

Even a small transaction or subscription cost to individual users will greatly deter users. Web sites that require registration or charge small fees for access have low levels of subscription and find that users are unwilling to purchase access. *USA Today* and *Encyclopaedia Britannica* are only two of many examples of online information services that users initially were required to pay for to get access. Usage for these web sites was well below expectations and both companies, like many others, determined that more revenue could be made through eliminating the barriers of access and creating greater advertising revenues.

A simple economic model can be used to show the effect of transaction costs on use of digital information over a network. Table 14.1 shows the benefit to four patrons from access to a scholarly journal. Each patron has the same benefit from the journal. Of these four patrons, Elizabeth has a higher opportunity cost of using the library's subscription. Elizabeth may have a higher salary than the other three patrons or may live farther from the library. Each patron also has a $5 transaction cost from purchasing an individual subscription. This is the cost of paying the subscription bill, having shelf space for the journal, and making certain every issue is received.

	Table 14.1 **Value of Print Subscription**			
	Benefit	**Opportunity Cost of Using the Library's Subscription**	**Transaction Cost of an Individual Subscription**	**Maximum Individual Subscription Price**
Elizabeth	$100	$60	$5	$55
Greg	$100	$20	$5	$15
James	$100	$20	$5	$15
George	$100	$20	$5	$15

The maximum subscription price a publisher can charge a patron is the opportunity cost of using the library minus the transaction cost of an individual subscription. If the publisher charges more than this, the individual will receive more benefit from the library's subscription than from a personal subscription. The publisher also charges the library a subscription price based on the total value patrons receive from it minus the opportunity cost of using the library. In this example, the publisher can charge up to $240 to the library for a subscription; the $80 value for each of three patrons. The publisher can charge Elizabeth $55 and receive a total revenue of $295.

In a digital, networked environment, the opportunity cost of access to the information decreases. Assume that this opportunity cost decreases to $0. In this case the publisher can charge the library the value of the subscription to the patrons, which equals $400. Selling individual subscriptions no longer makes sense because patrons can use the networked subscription at no cost. In addition, the transaction cost deters the publisher from charging individual patrons.

It is economically more efficient for the library to purchase a subscription license that enables it to share the subscription. This adds value to the library's subscription while removing individual paid subscribers to this journal. The publisher must increase the annual fee for access to the journal to match the demand increases from library patrons and the decreased revenue from individual subscriptions.

The change in library subscription fees also depends on the change in publisher costs. It is possible that decreasing costs of electronic journal publishing may decrease pricing of electronic journals. However, most of the costs of publishing in print and electronic format—editing, author's costs—are the same, with the exception of the costs of print distribution. It is unlikely that an elimination of print distribution costs would have a significant impact on pricing.

The transaction costs of billing and selecting journal titles also imply that there is an economic incentive for publishers to bundle access to journal titles available over the network. Electronic journal publishers frequently bundle subscriptions to electronic journals and offer different subscription contracts to libraries based on the number of journals in the bundle. This decreases publisher costs of billing for the bundle of titles rather than for individual titles and is another example of value-based pricing of journals.

Figure 14.1 shows a library's downward-sloping demand for journal titles. For any library, journal titles can be ranked from those titles that provide the most value to the library patrons to those that provide the least value, resulting in a downward-sloping demand for individual titles.

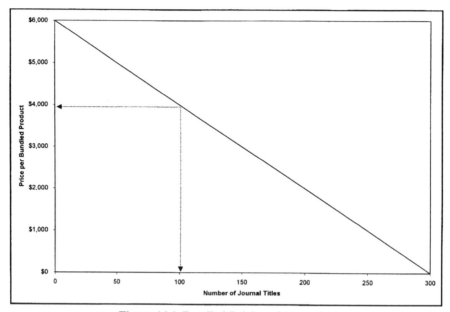

Figure 14.1. Bundled Pricing of Journals.

If Figure 14.1 accurately reflects the demand for journal titles by a library, then the publisher can get more profit by bundling the titles and charging a price for the bundle than by charging a single subscription price or by charging individual prices for individual titles. The bundled price eliminates the title-by-title decision of an acquisitions librarian. If the publisher charged $4,000 for access to each subscription individually, this library would subscribe to 100 titles. The publisher would receive $400,000 in revenue and the library would receive $100,000 in consumer surplus. Alternatively, the publisher can charge a bundled price of $500,000 for access to 100 titles. If the library is not able to purchase titles at $4,000 each, the library will purchase the bundle of 100 titles. In fact, the publisher would maximize profits by charging the library $900,000 for access to all 300 titles.

This assumes that there is no additional cost to the publisher of providing access to an additional title. This is true for electronic journals in a networked environment. Whether the publisher provides access to one-third of the database of journals or the entire database, there is no extra cost to the publisher. The publisher must determine the value the library receives from access to the database or to a part of the database.

The value or demand for access can be approximated by the number of patrons, size of the university or college, number of simultaneous users, or size of university endowment. Once library patrons are able to access the journal database, the use of journals is recorded electronically, enabling publishers to more precisely determine demand for individual titles and for the bundle of journal titles. The price of access to the database can then be changed based on a more precise measure of demand.

Because bundled pricing is more profitable than pricing journals title by title, there is an economic incentive for publishers to collect more e-journal titles. The more titles the publisher has in its portfolio of journals, the more likely it is that a library's patrons may use one of the titles, and the greater the potential revenue from the library. Because there is a difference in cost to the publisher between providing a library with access to one electronic journal and to 1,000 journals, the publisher with more electronic titles is more likely to collect higher access fees from library subscriptions. In addition, publishers have an economic incentive to merge, creating larger collections of electronic titles to bundle into subscriptions.

Role of Libraries in a Networked Environment

Just as publishers are likely to merge, customers of publishers also have an economic incentive to merge, forming a consortium. When this happens, the demand for journal use increases. Publishers can charge a higher price based on the greater value of the journal database. However, the negotiating ability of a consortium of subscribers may enable the consortium to negotiate a better price than the consortium members could get individually.

Value-based pricing is a negotiation between suppliers and demanders. Publishers can charge a price equal to the value of the bundle of journals. This price is unrelated to costs. It is possible that costs are comparable to the level of consumer benefit. However, the production cost does not influence the price. Libraries can pay less than their value from the bundle if they have sufficient bargaining power or negotiating skills to control the price. A consortium of libraries is likely to have stronger negotiating power collectively than do libraries individually.

As members of consortia or individually, there is an economic role for academic, public, and corporate libraries in providing purchasing, organizing, and distributing information in a networked environment. Transaction costs or the opportunity cost of finding information and making an economic transaction make it economically more efficient for the library to perform this societal role. Search engines and directories perform the role of finding and providing access to some information sources. However, information with scholarly value is likely to be provided only with the purchase of a license or subscription. When this happens, the library is an economically efficient venue for purchasing access to the information.

When information has sufficient value to be purchased, intellectual property laws endow the supplier with monopoly rights. As successful publishers build larger portfolios of electronic information, these monopoly rights become more valuable and more concentrated. Consumers become locked-in to the electronic subscription to a title and libraries become locked-in to subscriptions to bundles of titles.

As networked electronic information sources become more common and more valuable, libraries will find that they have less influence and power over their subscription fees. It is unlikely that any library or consortium will be able to cancel a subscription to the bundle of titles from a publisher. Patrons of these libraries will not accept cancellation of the electronic bundle of titles. If publishers want to maximize profits, the licenses for electronic bundles of titles enable them to raise subscription fees substantially. Therefore, prices for subscriptions to individual titles and to bundles of titles are likely to increase more significantly than they have in the past.

Summary

Digital information available over a network decreases the costs of distribution and reproduction. This does not change the value of the information, but does change the cost of providing it and may change the structure of contracts between publishers and consumers. Bundling of journal titles and merging of publishers is likely to increase as network access to digital information becomes more prevalent. In this environment, information users are likely to be locked-in to fewer sources of quality, scholarly information even while the amount of information users have access to increases. As a result, online publishers will have more market power than in the print environment.

Even though the cost of providing information may decrease, the demand or value from access to the information will increase. Intellectual property laws ensure that providers of information have ownership over it. Although the value of any single piece of information, or journal title, may decrease, ownership of larger stocks of information databases, journal titles, and other resources will collectively offer greater value to organizations such as libraries that serve as intermediaries between online publishers and users.

Bibliography

Akerlof, George A. "The Market for 'Lemons': Quality Uncertainty and the Market Mechanism." *Quarterly Journal of Economics* 84, no. 3 (August 1970): 488-500.

Ardis, Susan, and Karen S. Croneis. "Document Delivery, Cost Containment and Serial Ownership." *College & Research Libraries News* (November 1987): 624.

Besser, Howard. "Digital Image Distribution: A Study of Costs and Uses." *D-Lib Magazine* (October 1999). Available: http://www.dlib.org/dlib/october99/10besser.html. (Accessed January 8, 2001.

Bonk, Sharon C., and Dennis Pilling. "Modelling the Economics of Interlending." *Interlending & Document Supply* (April 1990): 52-56.

Bonn, Maria S., Wendy P. Lougee, Jeffrey K. MacKie-Mason, and Juan F. Riveros. "A Report on the PEAK Experiment." *D-Lib Magazine* (June 1999). Available: http://www.dlib.org/dlib/june99/06bonn.html. (Accessed January 8, 2001).

Bot, Marjolein, Johan Burgemeester, and Hans Roes. "The Cost of Publishing an Electronic Journal: A General Model and a Case Study." *D-Lib Magazine* (November 1998). Available: http://www.dlib.org/dlib/november98/11roes.html. (Accessed January 8, 2001).

Bowen, William G. "JSTOR and the Economics of Scholarly Communication." *Journal of Library Administration* 26, nos. 1/2 (December 1998): 27-44.

Braunstein, Yale M. "Resolving Conflicts Between Information Ownership and Intellectual Freedom." *Library Trends* (Summer–Fall 1990): 126-31.

Butler, Meredith, and Bruce Kingma, eds. *The Economics of Information in the Networked Environment*. Washington, DC: Association of Research Libraries, 1996.

Chressanthis, George A., and June D. Chressanthis. "A General Econometric Model of the Determinants of Library Subscription Prices of Scholarly Journals: The Role of Exchange Rate Risk and Other Factors." *Library Quarterly* 64, no. 3 (1994): 270-93.

———. "Publisher Monopoly Power and Third-Degree Price Discrimination of Scholarly Journals." *Technical Services Quarterly* (1993): 13-36.

———. "The Relationship Between Manuscripts Submission Fees and Journal Quality." *The Serials Librarian* (1993): 71-86.

Conway, Paul. "Yale University Library's Project Open Book: Preliminary Research Findings." *D-Lib Magazine* (February 1996). Available: http://www.dlib.org/dlib/february96/yale/02conway.html. (Accessed January 8, 2001).

Cox, John E. "The Changing Economic Model of Scholarly Publishing: Uncertainty, Complexity, and Multimedia Serials." *Library Acquisitions: Practice and Theory* 22, no. 2 (June 1998): 161-66.

Cummings, Martin M. "Cost Analysis: Methods and Realities." *Library Administration & Management* (Fall 1989): 181-83.

———. *The Economics of Research Libraries*. Washington, DC: Council on Library Resources, 1986.

Day, Colin. "The Economics of Publishing: The Consequences of Library and Research Copying." *Journal of the American Society for Information Science* 50, no. 4 (1999): 1346-49.

Due, R.T. "The Value of Information." *Information Systems Management* 13, no. 1 (Winter 1996): 68-72.

El-Hadidy, B. "The Breakeven Point for Using CD-ROM Versus Online. A Case Study for Database Access in a Developing Country." *Journal of the American Society for Information Science* 45, no. 4 (1994): 273-83.

Getz, Malcolm. "Depository Libraries and the Economics of Electronic Information." *The Bottom Line* (1987): 39-40.

———. "Economics: Document Delivery." *The Bottom Line* (Winter 1991–1992): 40-44.

———. "Economics: Electronic Information; Storage, Communication, and Access." *The Bottom Line* (1988): 39-40.

———. "Economics: Equity." *The Bottom Line* (Spring 1992): 45-46.

———. "Economics: How Journals Are Priced." *The Bottom Line* (1988): 37-39.

———. "Economics: Increasing the Value of User Time." *The Bottom Line* (1987): 37-39.

———. "Economics: National Research and Education Network." *The Bottom Line* (1989): 32-35.

———. "Economics: Pricing Photocopies." *The Bottom Line* (1987): 43-45.

———. "Economics: Storage Technologies." *The Bottom Line* (Spring 1990): 25-31.

———. "Electronic Publishing: An Economic View." *Serials Review* (1992): 25-31.

————. "Electronic Publishing in Academia: An Economic Perspective." *Serials Librarian* 36, nos. 1/2 (June 18, 1999): 263-300.

————. "More Benefits of Automation" *College & Research Libraries* (1988): 534-44.

————. "Some Benefits of the Online Catalog." *College & Research Libraries* (May 1987): 224-40.

Giacoma, Pete. *The Fee or Free Decision: Legal, Economic, Political, and Ethical Perspectives for Public Libraries.* New York: Neal-Schuman, 1989.

Grycz, Czeslaw Jan. "Economic Models for Networked Information." *Serials Review* (1992): 11-136.

Gupta, Alok, Dale O. Stahl, and Andrew B. Whinston. "The Economics of Network Management." *Communications of the ACM* 42, no. 9 (September 1999): 57-63.

Guthrie, Kevin M. "JSTOR: From Project to Independent Organization." *D-Lib Magazine* (July/August 1997). Available: http://www.dlib.org/dlib/july97/07guthrie.html. (Accessed January 8, 2001).

Harless, David W., and Frank R. Allen. "Using the Contingent Valuation Method to Measure Patron Benefits of Reference Desk Service in an Academic Library." *College & Research Libraries* 60, no. 1 (January 1999): 56-69.

Hegenbart, Barbara. "The Economics of the Internet Public Library." *Library Hi-Tech Journal* 16, no. 2 (June 1998): 69-83.

Herman, Edward S. "The Externalities Effects of Commercial and Public Broadcasting." In *The Political Economy of the Media. Volume 1,* edited by Peter Golding and Graham Murdock. Williston, VT: Elgar, 1997, 374-404.

Hunter, Karen. "Electronic Journal Publishing: Observations from Inside." *D-Lib Magazine* (July/August 1998). Available: http://www.dlib.org/dlib/july98/07hunter.html. (Accessed January 8, 2001).

Jackson, Mary E. "Library to Library: Fitting the Bill." *Wilson Library Bulletin* (June 1992): 95-97.

————. *Measuring the Performance of Interlibrary Loan and Document Delivery Services.* (December 1997). Available: http://www.arl.org/access/illdd-res/articles/illdd-res-measperf9712.shtml. (Accessed January 8, 2001).

Kantor, Paul B. "Library Cost Analysis." *Library Trends* (Fall 1989): 171-88.

————. "Three Studies of the Economics of Academic Libraries." *Advances in Library Administration and Organization* (1986): 221-86.

Kauffman, Robert J., and Frederick J. Riggins. "Information Systems and Economics." *Communications of the ACM* 41 (August 1998): 32-34.

Kenney, Anne R. (1997). *Digital to Microfilm Conversion: A Demonstration Project 1994–1996.* [Online]. Available: http://www.library.cornell.edu/ preservation/publications.html. (Accessed January 8, 2001).

King, D. W., and J. M. Griffiths. "Economic Issues Concerning Electronic Publishing and Distribution of Scholarly Articles." *Library Trends* 43, no. 4 (1995): 713-40.

King, Donald W. "Pricing policies in academic libraries." *Library Trends* 28, no. 1 (1979): 47-62.

———. "Some Economic Aspects of the Internet." *Journal of the American Society for Information Science* 49, no. 11 (1998): 990-1002.

Kingma, Bruce R. "The Costs of Print, Fiche, and Digital Access: The Early Canadiana Online Project." *D-Lib Magazine* (February 2000). Available: http://www.dlib.org/dlib/february00/kingma/02kingma.html. (Accessed January 8, 2001).

———. "The Economics of Access Versus Ownership: The Costs and Benefits of Access to Scholarly Articles via Interlibrary Loan and Journal Subscriptions." *Journal of Library Administration* 26, nos. 1/2 (December 1998): 145-57.

———. "Interlibrary Loan and Resource Sharing: The Economics of the SUNY Express Consortium." *Library Trends* 45, no. 3 (Winter 1997): 518-30.

Kingma, Bruce R., and Philip B. Eppard. "Journal Price Escalation and the Market for Information: The Librarians' Solution." *College & Research Libraries* (November 1992): 523-35.

Kingma, Bruce R., and Suzanne Irving. *The Economics of Access versus Ownership to Scholarly Information.* Binghamton, NY: Haworth Press, 1996.

Kingma, Bruce R., and Natalia Mouravieva. "The Economics of Access Versus Ownership: The Library for Natural Sciences Russian Academy of Sciences." *Interlending & Document Supply* 28, no. 1 (2000): 20-26.

Kivijarvi, H., and T. Saarinen. "Investment in Information Systems and the Financial Performance of the Firm." *Information and Management* 28, no. 2 (1995): 143-63.

Koenig, Michael E. D., and Johanna Goforth. "Libraries and the Cost Recovery Imperative." *IFLA Journal* (1993): 261-79.

Kutz, Myer. "Distributing the Costs of Scholarly Journals: Should Readers Contribute?" *Serials Review* (1992): 73-74.

Kurzweil, Raymond. "The Economics of Innovation." *Library Journal* (October 1991): 54-55.

Lamberton, D. M. "The Economics of Information and Organization." *Annual Review of Information Science and Technology* (1984): 3-30.

Lewis, David W. "Economics of the Scholarly Journal." *College & Research Libraries* (November 1989): 674-88.

————. "Why Books Are Bought and Borrowed." *The Bottom Line* (1988): 21-24.

Love, J. "Pricing Government Information." *Journal of Government Information* 22, no. 5 (1995): 363-87.

Machlup, Fritz. *The Economics of Information and Human Capital.* Princeton, NJ: Princeton University Press, 1984.

————. *Knowledge and Knowledge Production.* Princeton, NJ: Princeton University Press, 1980.

————. "Publishing Scholarly Books and Journals: Is It Economically Viable?" *Journal of Political Economy* (1977): 217-25.

————. "Stocks and Flows of Knowledge." *Kyklos* (1979): 400-11.

Mackie-Mason, J. K., and A. L. L. Jankovich. "PEAK: Pricing Electronic Access to Knowledge." *Library Acquisitions: Practice and Theory* 21, no. 3 (Fall 1997): 281-95.

Mackie-Mason, Jeffrey K., and Hal R. Varian. "Economic FAQs about the Internet." In *Internet Economics,* edited by Lee W. Knight and Joseph P. Bailey. Cambridge and London: MIT Press, 1997, 27-62.

————. "Pricing the Internet." In *Public Access to the Internet,* edited by Brian Kahin and James Keller. Cambridge and London: MIT Press, 1995, 269-314.

————. "Some Economics of the Internet." In *Networks, Infrastructure, and the New Task for Regulation,* edited by Werner Sichel and Donald L. Alexander. Ann Arbor: University of Michigan Press, 1996, 107-36.

MacKie-Mason, Jeffrey K., Liam Murphy, and John Murphy. "Responsive Pricing in the Internet." *Internet Economics,* edited by Lee W. Knight and Joseph P. Bailey. Cambridge and London: MIT Press, 1997, 279-303.

McCain, Roger A. "Information as Property and as a Public Good: Perspectives from the Economic Theory of Property Rights." *The Library Quarterly* (July 1988): 265-82.

McKnight, Lee W., and Joseph P. Bailey, eds. *Internet Economics.* Cambridge and London: MIT Press, 1997.

McPherson, Michael. "The Economics of University Investments in Information Resources." *Journal of Library Administration* 26, nos. 1/2 (December 1998): 73-77.

Mincer, Jacob. *Schooling, Experience, and Earnings.* New York: Columbia University Press, 1974.

Noll, Roger. "The Economics of Information." *Journal of Library Administration* 26, nos. 1/2 (December 1998): 47-55.

Noll, Roger, and W. Edward Steinmueller. "An Economic Analysis of Scientific Journal Prices: Preliminary Results." *Serials Review* (1992): 32-37.

O'Donnell, James. "Can E-journals Save Us? A Scholar's View." *Journal of Library Administration* 26, nos. 1/2 (December 1998): 181-86.

Peters, Paul-Evans. "Cost Centers and Measures in the Networked Information Value-Chain." *Journal of Library Administration* 26, nos. 1/2 (December 1998): 203-12.

Petersen, H. Craig. "The Economics of Economics Journals: A Statistical Analysis of Pricing Practices by Publishers." *College & Research Libraries* (March 1992): 176-81.

Rebarcak, P. Z., and D. Morris. "The Economics of Monographs Acquisitions. A Time/Cost Study Conducted at Iowa State University." *Library Acquisitions: Practice and Theory* 20, no. 1 (Spring 1996): 65-76.

Reed-Scott, Jutta. "Scholarship, Research Libraries, and Global Publishing: Economics of International Research Resources." *Journal of Library Administration* 27, nos. 3/4 (June 1999): 41-48.

Repo, Aatto J. "Economics of Information." *Annual Review of Information Science and Technology* (1987): 3-35.

———. "The Value of Information: Approaches in Economics, Accounting, and Management Science." *Journal of the American Society for Information Science* (March 1989): 68-85.

Riner, H. "Information Economics in the Internet Age." *Proceedings of the Eighteenth National Online Meeting* (1997): 287-94.

Rowley, J. "Principles of Price and Pricing Policy for the Information Marketplace." *Library Review* 46, no. 3 (1997): 179-89.

Ryan, James H. "Measuring Costs and Benefits of Distance Learning." *Journal of Library Administration* 26, nos. 1/2 (1998): 235-46.

Saffady, William. "The Availability and Cost of Online Search Services." *Library Technology Reports* (March/April 1992): 115-268.

Sairamesh, J., C. Nikolaou, D. F. Ferguson, and Y. Yemini. "Economic Framework for Pricing and Charging in Digital Libraries." *D-Lib Magazine* (February 1996). Available: http://www.dlib.org/dlib/february96/forth/02sairamesh.html. (Accessed January 8, 2001).

Schauer, Bruce P. *The Economics of Managing Library Service.* Chicago: American Library Association, 1986.

Shapiro, Carl, and Hal R. Varian. *Information Rules: A Strategic Guide to the Network Economy.* Boston: Harvard Business School Press, 1999.

Sharma, Khem R., Leung Ping Sun., and Lynn Zane. "Performance Measurement of Hawaii State Public Libraries: An Application of Data Envelopment Analysis (DEA)." *Agricultural and Resource Economics Review* (October 1999): 190-98.

Simpson, Donald B. "Library Consortia and Access to Information: Costs and Cost Justification." *Journal of Library Administration* (1990): 83-97.

Spence, Michael A. "An Economist's View of Information." In *Annual Review of Information Science and Technology,* vol. 9, edited by Carlos A. Cuadra and Ann W. Luke. Washington, DC: American Society for Information Science, 1974, 57-78.

———. "Job Market Signaling." *Quarterly Journal of Economics* 83, no. 3 (August 1973): 355-74.

Stoller, M. A., R. Christopherson and M. Miranda. "The Economics of Professional Journal Pricing." *College and Research Libraries* 57, no. 1 (1996): 9-21.

Tenopir, Carol. "Pricing Options." *Library Journal* 122, no. 14 (September 1998): 130-32.

———. "Should We Cancel Print?" *Library Journal* 124, no. 14 (September 1999): 138-42.

Tenopir, Carol, and Donald W. King. *Towards Electronic Journals: Realities for Scientists, Librarians, and Publishers.* Washington, DC: Special Library Association Publishing, 2000.

———. "Trends in Scientific Scholarly Journal Publishing in the United States." *Journal of Scholarly Publishing* (April 1997): 135-70.

Van House, Nancy A. *Public Library User Fees.* Westport, CT: Greenwood, 1983.

———. "Research on the Economics of Libraries." *Library Trends* (Spring 1984): 407-23.

Varian, Hal R. "The Economics of the Internet and Academia." *Journal of Library Administration* 26, nos. 1/2 (December 1998): 57-71.

———. "Pricing Electronic Journals." *D-Lib Magazine* (June 1996). Available: http://www.dlib.org/dlib/june96/06varian.html. (Accessed January 8, 2001).

Varlejs, Jana, ed, *The Economics of Information in the 1990s.* Jefferson, NC: McFarland, 1995.

Wolpert, Samuel A., and Joyce Friedman Wolpert. *Economics of Information.* New York: Van Nostrand Reinhold, 1986.

Woodsworth, Anne, and James F. Williams. *Managing the Economics of Owning, Leasing and Contracting out Information Services.* Brookfield, VT: Ashgate, 1993.

Index

Access fees. *See* User fees
Accounting, managerial
　　break-even analysis, 3
　　cost analysis, 3
　　performance analysis, 3
Advertising
　　for financing public goods, 64, 110
Allocation mechanisms, 1, 45, 113–16
Asymmetrical information in markets
　　in general, 92–95
　　in information markets, 95–98
　　solutions to, 94–95
Average cost
　　defined, 12
　　in sample cases, 13–14, 17, 81–82,
　　　　108, 154

Benefit(s). *See also* Marginal benefits
　　from books and journals, 104
　　collective, 103–4, 141–43
　　and demand, 29–30
　　from digital information, 151, 155,
　　　　161
　　estimating without a market, 46
　　and externalities, 65–66, 68
　　in general, 2
　　of information acquisition, 98–101
　　of junk mail, 67, 70–72
　　manager's perceptions of, 4
　　and present value, 138
　　from public goods, 58–59
　　quantifying, 4, 60
　　time saved, 130–31
　　from used cars, 92–95
　　and willingness-to-pay, 29–30, 53, 68
Books and journals. *See also*
　　　　Information goods and services
　　benefits from, 104
　　demand for, 104
Break-even analysis, 3

Cable service
　　as example of natural monopoly, 81
Commodities. *See* Private goods
Complementary goods and services,
　　33–35
Congestion
　　opportunity cost of, 133–35
Consortia, 142, 145–47. *See also*
　　　　Resource sharing
Consumer income
　　effect on demand, 30, 32–33
Consumer surplus, 3
　　in competitive market, 78
　　as deadweight loss, 78
　　defined, 40
　　from digital information, 151
　　and economic cost, 132–33
　　illustrated, 40–43
　　from junk mail, 71
　　from library services, 119–21, 133
　　and multi-price suppliers, 85–87
　　from photocopying services, 138–39
　　from resource sharing, 147
Consumer tastes
　　effect on demand, 30, 35
Consumer theory, 29
Copyright
　　creating monopoly control over
　　　　information goods, 76, 82
　　and financing of public goods,
　　　　110
　　and the Internet, 63
Cost analysis, 3
Cost structure of information goods
　　differences from cost structure of
　　　　classic goods, 17
Cost structure of organization
　　categories of costs in, 15
　　and organizational goals, 9

Cost(s). *See also* Average cost; Fixed
    costs; Marginal costs; Total cost;
    Variable costs
  and benefits, 30
  defined, 9
  estimating without a market, 46
  in general, 1
  of information acquisition, 98–99
  of information goods and services,
    128
  manager's perceptions of, 4
  and present value, 138
  of producing unit of output, 9
  quantifying, 4, 9
  of resource sharing, 141, 146
  and supply, 21–23
  of using interlibrary loan, 131
Cost-benefit analysis, 2, 3
  of information markets, 4
  and marginal cost, 3
  and opportunity costs, 19, 127–28
  and producer surplus, 3
  and supply, 3

Deadweight loss, 78, 81–82, 84, 106,
    115–24, 139
Demand. *See also* Monopoly demand;
    Price elasticity of demand;
    Willingness-to-pay
  and benefit, 30
  for books and journals, 104–5, 143
  defined, 29
  for digital information, 157–58, 161,
    163–64
  for durable goods, 138
  effect of consumer tastes on, 30, 35
  effect of changes in consumer
    income on, 30, 32–33
  effect of number of consumers on,
    30, 35
  effect of price of good on, 30–32
  effect of prices of related goods on,
    30, 32
  effects on market equilibrium, 47–51
  elastic, 49–50
  estimating without a market, 45
  in general, 1, 3, 5
  inelastic, 37, 50, 63
  for interlibrary loan, 132
  law of, 30–31

for photocopying, 114–17
for public goods, 58–60
unit-elastic, 37
Digital information, 151. *See also*
    Network economics
  and average cost, 18
  benefits of, 151, 155, 157
  costs of
    consumer, 152–53
    intermediary, 154–56
    producer, 154–56
  keyword searching, 151
  and marginal costs, 18
  pricing, 156–58
Diminishing/declining marginal
    productivity
  described, 16–17
Donations
  for financing public goods, 61–62,
    110
Duopoly, defined, 76
Durable goods
  demand for, 138
  examples of, 97, 136

Economic efficiency, 4, 19, 121–22,
    144–45
  defined, 2, 142
  and market equilibrium, 51, 54, 75,
    87
  and monopolies, 77–79
  pareto optimum, 51–53, 75–76, 105
Economic inefficiency, 106
  caused by asymmetrical information,
    92, 96, 97
  defined, 2
Economics. *See also* Information
    economics
  defined, 1, 4
  and policy decisions, 3
  rationale for studying, 2-4
  as study of human behavior, 5-6
  tools for decision making, 1, 5
Elastic supply curve, 26, 47–48
Expectations, 90–91, 99–100
Externalities, 8. *See also* Negative
    externalities; Positive
    externalities
  balancing, 70–72

Fixed costs, 7. *See also* Average cost; Cost(s); Opportunity costs; Total cost; Variable costs
  allocated, 20
  categories of, 15
  defined, 10
  of digital information, 152–54, 158
  direct, 20
  economic, 20
  explicit, 20
  first-copy, 20, 81–82, 158
  implicit, 20
  indirect, 20
  life-cycle, 21
  nominal, 21
  overhead, 20
  real (inflation adjusted), 21
  in sample cases, 81, 108, 138–39, 142, 148
  sunk, 21
For-profit organizations
  goals of, 9

Good reputation, 94
Government agencies
  goals of, 9
Government regulation
  of goods and services having positive externalities, 69–70
Government subsidy
  of information goods and services, 70
Guarantees, 94

Inelastic supply curve, 27, 48–49
Inferior goods, 33. *See also* Normal goods; Related goods
Information acquisition
  benefits of, 98–101
  costs of, 98–99
  value of, 101
Information economics
  differences from classic economics, 6
Information goods and services. *See also* Books and journals; Cost structure of information goods; Digital information; Information acquisition; Information markets
  as complementary goods, 35
  cost-benefit analysis of, 128

  differences from classic goods and services, 7, 17
  financing, 70, 121–25
  fixed costs in production of, 17
  marginal costs in production of, 17
  and market failures, 54
  and negative externalities, 66–68
  opportunity costs and, 20, 128
  and positive externalities, 69–70
  price elasticity of demand for, 40
  as public goods, 7, 58, 63–64, 107
  and user fees, 120
Information managers
  and economic decisions, 1
Information markets, 5. *See also* Information acquisition; Information goods and services; Markets
  asymmetrical information in, 89–90, 95–98
  digital information, 4, 18, 151–59
  education, 97
  expectations in, 90–91
  externalities of. *See* Negative externalities; Positive externalities
  insurance, 96–97
  journal pricing and subscription policies, 4, 59–61, 75
  junk mail, 4, 66–68, 70–72
  employment, 97–98
  marriage, 97–98
  as monopolies. *See* Monopolies
  and public goods. *See* Public goods
  software, 108–10
  telephone service, 4, 5
Inputs
  and cost of producing unit of output, 9, 11
  fixed, 11, 17
  productivity of, 9
  quantifying, 9
  variable, 11, 16
Insurance markets, 96–97
Intellectual property, protecting, 82, 84, 165
Interlibrary loan services
  and opportunity costs, 19, 128, 131
  in resource sharing, 142–45, 147–49

Internet
  access, 153, 155
  and copyright violations, 63
  cost of congestion, 133–35
  as exclusionary public good, 61
  and opportunity costs, 19, 133, 153
  and user fees, 121

Journal subscriptions
  bundling of, 163–65
  as monopoly, 75
  pricing of, 123, 158, 162–65. *See
    also* Multi-price suppliers
  as public goods, sample case, 59–61
  in resource sharing, 142–43
Junk mail
  as example of negative externality,
    66–68
  as example of positive externality,
    70–72

"Law of the invisible hand," 45, 47
Lemon laws, 95

Marginal benefits, 3, 5. *See also*
    Benefit(s)
  from books and journals, 105–6
  and financing by donations, 62
  from interlibrary loan, 132
  from Internet use, 134–35
  from library computer network, 122–23
  marginal private benefit, 71
  marginal social benefit, 71
  from photocopying, 114–17
  from software, 109
Marginal costs, 3, 5. *See also* Average
    cost; Cost(s); Fixed costs;
    Opportunity costs; Total cost;
    Variable costs
  cost-benefit analysis and, 3
  defined, 12
  marginal cost pricing, 114–16
  marginal social cost, 67
  of patron time, 147–48
  of pricing, 117–21
  of resource sharing, 141
  in sample cases, 13–15, 17, 77,
      81–84, 87, 105, 108, 114–17,
      122, 134–35, 138, 154–55, 158
  and time, 12

Marginal revenue, 78, 81, 87
Market equilibrium. *See also* Market
    failure; Markets
  competitive, 79
  defined, 46
  and economic efficiency, 51
  effects of changes in demand and
    supply on, 47–51
  and externalities, 65
  illustrated, 46–47, 81
  and multi-price suppliers, 87
  and pareto optimum, 51–54, 75–76,
    105
Market failure. *See also* Market
    equilibrium; Markets
  categories of
    caused by asymmetrical/imperfect
      information, 55, 95–98
    externalities. *See* Externalities
    monopolies. *See* Monopolies
    public goods. *See* Public goods
  defined, 53
  examples of, 53–54
Markets. *See also* Information markets;
    Market equilibrium; Market
    failure
  asymmetrical information in, 92–95
  and the "law of the invisible hand,"
    45, 47
  noncompetitive. *See* Monopolies
Monopolies, 8. *See also* Duopoly;
    Monopoly demand; Monopsony;
    Natural monopolies; Oligopoly
  defined, 76
  examples of, 75, 77–80
  in information markets, 76, 80–85
Monopoly demand, 77–80
Monopoly pricing, 82–83
Monopsony, defined, 76
Multi-price suppliers, examples of,
    85–87, 124–25. *See also*
    Value-based pricing

Name brands, 94
Natural monopolies
  example of, 81
  defined, 80
Negative externalities, 65
  defined, 66
  examples of, 66–68, 133

Network economics, 161
 pricing electronic journals, 162–65
 role of libraries in network, 165–66
Nonprofit organizations
 and asymmetrical information, 94
 financing of, 62, 113
 goals of, 9
 and junk mail, 67
Non-rival goods and services, 57,
 133–34
Normal goods, 32. *See also* Information
 goods and services; Related
 goods
Number of consumers
 effect on demand, 35

Oligopoly, defined, 76
Opportunity costs, 20. *See also* Average
 cost; Cost(s); Fixed costs;
 Marginal costs; Total cost;
 Variable costs
 defined, 18, 20
 of digital information, 151–53,
 156–57, 161–63, 165
 of Internet use, 133–35, 153
 measuring, 129–30
 of negative externalities, 66
 of patron time, 142, 147–49
 of positive externalities, 69
 and public goods, 60
 value of time as, 19, 21, 66, 69,
 127–39
Organizational goals
 and cost structure, 9
Output, 9
 and average cost, 12, 14
 benefits of, 9
 and changes in price, 25
 determining level of, 9, 60, 78, 104
 effects of changes in level of, 10, 15,
 18, 84
 and fixed costs, 18
 and marginal costs, 12, 18, 25
 pareto optimum, 51–53
 profit-maximizing quantity, 78
 quantifying, 9

Pareto optimum, 51–54, 75–76, 105
Perfectly elastic demand curve, 38
Perfectly inelastic demand curve, 38
Performance analysis, 3
Photocopying
 as pricing example, 114–17, 121–22,
 138–39
Policy decisions
 and economics, 3
Pollution
 as example of market failure, 53–54
Positive externalities, 65
 defined, 68
 example of, 69
 government support/regulation of
 goods and services having,
 69–70
Present value, 136–39
Price. *See also* Market equilibrium;
 Multi-price suppliers; Price
 elasticity of demand
 as allocation mechanism, 45, 113–16
 of digital information, 156–58,
 162–65
 effect on demand, 30–32, 35–40
 and externalities, 65
 as financing mechanism, 116
 marginal cost of pricing, 117–21
 network example, 122–23
 photocopying examples, 114–17,
 121–22, 138–39
 Ramsey, 114, 121–23, 139
 value-based, 114, 123–25, 156–58,
 161, 163, 165
Price elasticity of demand, 49–51. *See
 also* Price elasticity of supply
 defined/measured, 35–40
 in sample case, 119–20
Price elasticity of supply, 47–49. *See
 also* Price elasticity of demand
 defined, 25–26
 perfectly elastic supply curve, 26
 perfectly inelastic supply curve, 27
Price-taker, 22, 27
Private goods/commodities
 contrasted with public goods, 57,
 103–10
 financing of, 104, 113

Producer surplus, 3
Public goods
    contrasted with private
        goods/commodities, 57,
        103–10
    demand for, 58–60, 106
    exclusionary, 61
    financing of, 58, 61–64, 103, 107, 110
    information as, 7–8, 58, 63–64
    journal subscriptions, sample case,
        59–61
    nonexclusionary, 62–64
    resource sharing as, 141
Public libraries
    benefits provided to community, 3
    financing of, 62

Ramsey pricing, 114, 121–23, 139
Related goods
    complements, 33–35
    substitutes, 33
Research Libraries Network (RLN), 147
Resource sharing
    benefits of, 141
    costs of, 141
    defined, 141
    financing, 147
    multiple users of resources, 141–47
    opportunity cost of patron time, 147–49
    as public good, 141
Risk. *See* Uncertainty and risk

Shared goods. *See* Public goods
Smith, Adam, 45, 47
Software markets, 108–10
    pricing example, 123–24
Substitute goods, 33
    elastic goods, 39
Supply. *See also* Price elasticity of supply
    and costs, 21–23
    curves, 77, 104–5
    effects on market equilibrium, 47–51
    in general, 1, 5
    market supply, 23–25

Tax revenue
    for financing public goods, 61, 110
    and nonexclusionary public goods, 62
Telephone installation/service
    benefit from, 5

as example of monopoly, 77–80
Time. *See* Value of time
Total cost
    in sample case, 13

Uncertainty and risk, 89
    adverse selection, 96
    asymmetrical information, 92–98
    expectations, 90–91
    moral hazard, 96
    risk neutrality, 99
Used car market
    as example of asymmetrical
        information, 92–95
User fees
    as allocation tools, 114–16
    cost of charging, 117–21
    for financing private goods, 113
    for financing public goods, 61, 110
    and the Internet, 135
    for network access, 165

Value of information
    effect of timing on, 7, 110
    expected value, 91, 94, 100
Value of time, 19–21, 66, 69, 127
    congestion, 133–35
    measuring, 128–33
    patron time, 147–49
    present value, 136–39
Value-based pricing, 114, 123–25,
        156–58, 161, 163, 165
Variable costs. *See also* Average cost;
        Cost(s); Fixed costs; Opportunity
        costs; Total cost
    categories of, 15
    defined, 10
    of digital information, 152
    and level of output, 10, 15–16

Warranties, 94
Willingness-to-pay
    and benefit, 29–30, 53, 68
    defined, 29–30
    for information, 100–101, 106
    marginal, 79, 86–87
    and public goods, 58–59
    for software, 108
    for used cars, 92